Reading Shakespeare
Film First

Reading Shakespeare Film First

Mary Ellen Dakin
Revere High School
Revere, Massachusetts

Foreword by Alan B. Teasley

National Council of Teachers of English
1111 W. Kenyon Road, Urbana, Illinois 61801-1096

Staff Editor: Bonny Graham

Interior Design: Doug Burnett

Cover Design: Pat Mayer

Cover Images: iStockphoto.com/Artpilot; iStockphoto.com/iLexx

NCTE Stock Number: 39073

©2012 by the National Council of Teachers of English.

It is the policy of NCTE in its journals and other publications to provide a forum for the open discussion of ideas concerning the content and the teaching of English and the language arts. Publicity accorded to any particular point of view does not imply endorsement by the Executive Committee, the Board of Directors, or the membership at large, except in announcements of policy, where such endorsement is clearly specified.

Every effort has been made to provide URLs that were accurate when the text was written, but because of the rapidly changing nature of the Web, some sites and addresses may no longer be accessible.

Library of Congress Cataloging-in-Publication Data

Dakin, Mary Ellen, 1952–
    Reading Shakespeare film first / Mary Ellen Dakin; foreword by Alan B. Teassley.
        p. cm.
    Includes bibliographical references and index.
    ISBN 978-0-8141-3907-3 (pbk.)
    1. Shakespeare, William, 1564–1616—Study and teaching (Secondary) 2. Shakespeare, William, 1564–1616—Film adaptations. I. Title.
    PR2987.D34 2013
    822.3'3—dc23
                                                                    2012028605

To students in the 2010–2012 Shakespeare elective:

From the rough magic of our working days these pages came to be . . .

Edward Adams	Marissa Maccioli
Alexa Amore	Kendall MacDonald
Lauren Armstrong	Xuyen Mai
Kelly Avalos	Diego Mancia
Edwin Ayala	Lillian McKinley
Yasmen Bellemsieh	Adriana Meadowcroft
Kannika Chap	Javier Muñoz
Jeffrey Chhay	Rachel Murray
Lindsay Chorlian	Kelsey Nazzaro
Steven Crowe	Taylor Oliva
Guil DeAndrade	Juliana Panzini
Sophia DesJardins	Jordan Rodriguez
Nanci DiLiegro	Heather Romancito
Jonathan Esmurria	Jennifer Sao
Kate Ferrante	Jimmy Sherman
Lynsdale Ford	Gianna Tamburello
Lizzy Gordon	Estrella Vargas
Yosselin Guzman	Elma Velic
Chanyce Kane	Charlie Wongwajarachot
Aaron Leon	Jenelle Worcester
Glenda Lopez	

. . . And beyond measure to my children, Michael, Brian, and Beth, who first taught me to see through digitized eyes the future in the past.

Contents

Whether the primary focus in a Shakespeare unit is on
Shakespeare as literary and theatrical text or Shakespeare
as film, when the introduction to fundamental concepts of
visual composing is grounded in images of the play they
are about to read or view, students enter two new worlds
at once—the world of film and the world of Shakespeare's
play. This chapter sets the stage for each consecutive chapter
in the book.

Selling tickets has come a long way since William Shakespeare vied for box office success. As consumers of art and
entertainment in a twenty-first-century audience, students
need to make meaning from a variety of texts composed for
not only artistic but also commercial purposes. This chapter
builds on the elements of visual composition set forth in
Chapter 1 and outlines a dynamic process of reading the
rhetoric of Shakespeare film posters, publicity stills, and film
trailers.

This chapter introduces students to the construct of Shakespeare's three faces—literary, theatrical, and cinematic—and
to the ways in which Shakespeare's literary and theatrical text
is transmediated into film. The viewing strategies introduced
here establish a foundation for reading Shakespeare *with* film
and *on* film that informs every teaching scenario.

Permission Acknowledgments

Film photos courtesy of Photofest, 32 East 31st Street, 5th Fl., New York, New York 10016.

Film poster images courtesy of the Movie Poster Data Base, www.learnabout movieposters.com/newsite/movies/MPDB.asp.

Page 78: Plot line for *Romeo and Juliet* in Figure 6.3 adapted from the New Folger Library Shakespeare edition of the play edited by Barbara A. Mowat and Paul Werstine (Washington Square Press, 1992). Reprinted by permission of the Folger Shakespeare Library.

Page 86: "Critical Film Review" list adapted from *Great Films and How to Teach Them* by William V. Costanzo (p. 299, National Council of Teachers of English, 2004). Copyright 2004 by the National Council of Teachers of English.

Page 88: Figure 7.1 chart adapted from "Where to Be or Not to Be: The Question of Place in *Hamlet*" by John Golden (*English Journal* 99.1, 2009). Copyright 2009 by the National Council of Teachers of English.

Page 137: Formatting for Handout 7.1, *Henry V* viewing guide, reprinted and adapted with permission from *Reel Conversations: Reading Films with Young Adults* by Alan B. Teasley and Ann Wilder. Copyright © 1997 by Alan B. Teasley and Ann Wilder. Published by Boynton/Cook, Portsmouth, NH. All rights reserved.

Foreword

I can now admit that, as a high school English teacher, I was ambivalent about teaching Shakespeare. I knew that I *should* teach Shakespeare; I even *wanted* to teach Shakespeare. I just couldn't bear the looks on the students' faces when I would say, "Our next unit is a Shakespeare play. It will be exciting. It is important. You'll be a better person because we do this. Really!" In some years, we navigated *Hamlet* without too many scars—*Macbeth* not so much. In my world, at least, the melancholy Dane was an easier sell than the murderous Thane, even with the witches. My seniors liked *The Taming of the Shrew* because it was the only comic work we read the entire year other than "A Modest Proposal," and they didn't really find Swift's proposal all that funny.

I used the best techniques I could come up with, mostly aping my college professors. Usually I would provide what I considered necessary background information (Shakespeare's Life, the Elizabethan Period, the Globe Theatre), the students would read scenes aloud (without rehearsal and without expression), and every few lines I would ask them what they thought it meant. If they were silent for much longer than ten seconds, I'd cave in and *tell* them What It Meant, so we could move on. If I lucked into an effective strategy, I'd probably use it again the following year. Looking back on the experience, I see that I had no theoretical framework to guide me, much less any coherent ideas about instruction. I taught Shakespeare like I taught everything else—as a Text We Would Analyze Together. Students would be engaged. I would will it so.

What I needed was the work of Mary Ellen Dakin.

If you have read Mary Ellen's first book, *Reading Shakespeare with Young Adults* (NCTE, 2009), the wealth of terrific teaching ideas in this book will not surprise you. What may surprise you is how perfectly *Reading Shakespeare Film First* addresses so many of the challenges of teaching English in the chilly new world of twenty-first-century content and skills, Common Core State Standards, standardized tests, increasing calls for academic rigor, and students distracted by media overload. After all, how can we hope to do Shakespeare justice in a linguistic environment in which *text, message,* and *friend* are accepted as verbs? How can we seriously explore hamartia when the word *tragedy* is used to describe everything from a celebrity divorce to a tornado?

When I first read the title of the current book, I admit I was skeptical. I liked the idea of using film to teach Shakespeare, but I was afraid the author was one of those teachers who use film *only* in the service of literature. You might even have had a colleague like that—one who would prefer that students interact only with words on a page, but who might deign to show part of a film version as a visual aid for the honors students or use *only* the film with the standard students because that was better than nothing. These colleagues might tolerate a film experience, but a reading experience was infinitely preferable. As a longtime media literacy advocate, I wanted no part of an approach that put film in a subservient role. However, I was also worried about the "film first" claim, fearing the scandalized traditionalists would immediately dismiss such a book. Mary Ellen might have ventured too far out of our collective comfort zone.

As I read the manuscript, however, I was immediately both relieved and impressed. Mary Ellen is the kind of reflective practitioner I so admire. She sets out with a huge commitment to engage her students in Shakespeare's plays and a few simple yet powerful ideas for applying the tools of media literacy to this purpose. She tries some strategies. She notices what's working. She refines the strategies. She shares her ideas with colleagues, and they then use and refine the strategies. You can see the momentum building around her. This is action research at its best: classroom innovation by thoughtful teachers, resulting in active learning by both students and teachers. And she pulls it off! She really does use media literacy best practices to teach the plays of Shakespeare, and she does so in ways that honor both media literacy and Shakespeare.

Best of all, Mary Ellen shows us how *we* can do it, too. She describes classroom scenarios vividly, allowing us to hear the voices of her students and colleagues as they find new ways to engage in Shakespeare and puzzle through challenging texts. Her students learn to view three faces of the plays—as literary, theatrical, and cinematic experiences—so our students can learn these skills, too. She shows us the process and provides us with the handouts to make the lessons work.

Oh dear! Now I've done it. You just turned to the back of the book, saw all the amazing handouts, stopped reading, and headed for the cash register (or, if you are online, you "added it to your cart" and clicked on "purchase"). Well, come back here a minute! There'll be time for that. Sure, you can use those handouts tomorrow at third period, but I'd recommend you also *read* the book—all of it—*from front to back*. You need to earn those handouts, my friend.

I love the structure of this book. Mary Ellen begins simply—analyzing movie posters and trailers as a way of building interest in the plays—and her strategies build in complexity from there. She explains in careful detail how to approach each of the three faces of film. Then she shows us great ways to use an entire film. By the time you get to the transmediation project in Chapter 8, you may feel the top of your head peeling back ever so slowly to make room for all of the new ideas you want to try out yourself.

This book fills a void we didn't know existed until Mary Ellen showed us the opportunities we were missing. She has shown us ways to use media literacy techniques—coupled with thoughtful exploration of interrelationships between text, theater, and film—to engage today's students in Shakespeare. Her strategies are impressive, her tips and coaching supremely useful.

Best of all, her love and appreciation of Shakespeare and her commitment to her students are evident on every page.

Alan B. Teasley
Duke University

Preface

The chapters of *Reading Shakespeare Film First* replicate the stages of a journey made by its author, her students, and colleagues, who set out in earnest several years ago to explore the brave new world of William Shakespeare's early modern English text transmediated into images, sound, and film, and who returned to our books as readers transformed. (For an examination of reading Shakespeare's printed text, begin with *Reading Shakespeare with Young Adults*, published by NCTE in 2009.) The eight chapters map a sequence of instructional practices designed to support students in the acquisition of both the language of film and the language of William Shakespeare's plays. The chapters evolve from teaching scenarios in which the balance of instruction shifts gradually from reading Shakespeare word first to reading Shakespeare film first.

The companion website, www.readingshakespeare.org, is designed to connect, extend, update, and animate the material in both books and to host a dynamic conversation about reading Shakespeare in the twenty-first century with all our students.

Introduction

. . . what's past is prologue, . . .
The Tempest 2.1.289

In the dark backward and abysm of time, a three-year-old girl stands in front of a small television screen transfixed by an old movie and the strange boy who won't obey the rules of being human. Filmed in black and white, he is all sparkle and haze. He laugh-speaks and he brays. *Who is this?* she wonders. One day she finds him beneath the kitchen table, visible only to her. For a short time, Puck is her friend. Then he vanishes and over the years he slumbers in memory, indistinct as a dream.

Fast-forward to a high school on the outskirts of Boston, Massachusetts. Now an English teacher, the grown-up girl suspects that if students can learn to read Shakespeare's language in all its magical complexity, the skills they master will transfer to their reading of literature and enrich their lives, and no child will be left behind. She brings Max Reinhardt's 1935 film production of *A Midsummer Night's Dream* into the classroom, thinking that the film will reward students with a retelling of the text, but she learns that the language of literature is compounded by the language of film. She understands now, as she writes this book, that even the most formalist productions of Shakespeare on film blaze a trail in directions Shakespeare never traveled, by means of sequential and variable frames, camera angles and movement, editing, densely detailed sets, lighting, special effects, and a highly interpretive sound track. Film is so much more than a retelling of a literary work; it is a *revision,* in the fullest sense of the word. Still, film does not speak in a language foreign to the brain; it is a native language unstudied and unschooled.

"We are born," biologist Lewis Thomas writes, "knowing how to use language" (105), and though it is barely one hundred years old, the language of film may be as innately decipherable to us as the language we learn in the womb. In his 1982 groundbreaking study of the foundations of cinema literacy, Stefan Sharff argues that "the ability to decipher and follow a cinema syntax resembles the innate faculty for language," though our comprehension of a "visual grammar is still tentative . . . and often unconscious" (2–3).

As we work with students on the literary and theatrical richness of Shakespeare's text, we can no longer relegate to the corners of consciousness the cinematic richness of Shakespeare on film. The potential for the mutual reinforcement and transfer of twenty-first-century literacy skills between text and film is too promising to overlook. This book is meant to guide teachers and students on a journey there and back again, with carefully researched and classroom-tested strategies for crossing over from Shakespeare's rich and strange early modern English to equally rich and strange modern film and graphic productions of his plays.

But the journey doesn't have to begin with words on the page; the journey can and sometimes should begin with images and film. "More movies have been based on Shakespeare's works," observes William Costanzo, author of *Great Films and How to Teach Them*, "than on any other writer's" (165). When Shakespeare is in the curriculum, and he usually is, we have an exciting opportunity to guide students in an exploration of what film scholar Judith Buchanan calls the "transmediation" of Shakespeare from the medium of literary script to screenplay and film. This book is the record of a sustained attempt to take Shakespeare into the twenty-first-century classroom and to learn from the convergence of old and new media why we continue to hold Shakespeare's mirror up to nature and see ourselves and our world new-framed.

We need to infuse our teaching with the rich complexity of text, language, and reading, terms used in their fullest sense throughout *Standards for the English Language Arts* published by the International Reading Association (IRA) and the National Council of Teachers of English (NCTE):

> Briefly, we use the term *text* broadly to refer not only to printed texts, but also to spoken language, graphics, and technological communications. *Language* as it is used here encompasses visual communication in addition to spoken and written forms of expression. And *reading* refers to listening and viewing in addition to print-oriented reading. (2)

This book began as the longest single chapter in a manuscript I submitted to NCTE in 2007 and removed before publication in 2009 because it did not thoroughly and thoughtfully answer all the questions I had about reading Shakespeare on film. I needed to learn much more about spoken and visual language, graphics, and technological communications. Beyond research and the crucible of practice, I hoped that the Common Core State Standards we now share with colleagues across content areas and state lines would break down the walls that divide us and foster meaningful collaborative learning. With patient guidance from editor Bonny Graham at NCTE, with thoughtful support from Robert Young, director of education at the Folger Shakespeare Library, and with constant help from colleagues and administrators throughout the

Revere Public Schools—Allison Giordano Casper, Althea Terenzi, Matt Despres, George Hannah, Kelly Chase, Tim Alperen, Bill Drewnowski, Nancy Barile, Sara Rice, and Antonio Cinelli in the English department; Mark Fellowes, Bill O'Brien, and Michael Bonanno in history; David Eatough, Axel Larson, and Erin Parker in science; Alec Waugh in music and technology; Nick Botto in special education; Director of Humanities Jonathan Mitchell; Principal Dr. Lourenco Garcia; Literacy Coach Christina Porter; Library Media Specialist Rachel Bouhanda; Audio-Video Specialist Paul Amato; Senior Associate at Great Schools Partnership Mary Hastings; photographer and former student Jennifer Cimino, artist and former student Jennifer Sao—the chapter became a book.

How should we read Shakespeare with all our students in the twenty-first century? It is the central argument of this book that we need to learn with our students how to read Shakespeare in triplicate, as the stuff of transformative literature, theater, and film. The combined effect will be greater than the sum of its parts. Our students will learn from the most frequently taught, most frequently performed, and most frequently filmed author in the English-speaking canon that language is malleable as clay and meaning is a shared construction, that performance is a dynamic act of selective reading, and that film is new-age hieroglyphics. It is our students who will construct the future paradigms of literature, rhetoric, and art. Let us prepare them.

Note: All handouts can be found in the appendix at the back of the book. Unless otherwise noted, all line citations in this book are from the Folger editions of the plays, edited by Barbara A. Mowat and Paul Werstine.

The Prologue

And as imagination bodies forth
The forms of things unknown, the poet's pen
Turns them to shapes and gives to airy nothing
A local habitation and a name.

A Midsummer Night's Dream 5.1.15–18

EXTERIOR / FOLGER SHAKESPEARE LIBRARY, WASHINGTON, DC / DAY
Teachers, students, scholars, filmmakers, and tourists walk along the marble exterior of the library, stopping occasionally to view the inscribed bas-reliefs before wandering inside. From within, the sound of voices, the white noise of public space, and intermittent silence acoustically reflect against the oak-paneled walls.

INTERIOR / GREAT HALL / DAY
Standing before an exhibit of posters and photographs from silent film productions of William Shakespeare's plays produced at the dawn of the twentieth century, scholar Deborah Cartmell speaks to a small group.

> *Cartmell:* The question we need to ask is, if we lose the words, do we lose '"Shakespeare"?

INTERIOR / ELIZABETHAN THEATRE / DAY
On the stage, film director Michael Almereyda stands before a large monitor projecting his 2000 film adaptation of Hamlet, *the audio muted. He speaks to a gathering crowd.*

> *Almereyda:* My main job was to imagine a parallel visual language that might hold a candle to Shakespeare's poetry.

INTERIOR / READING ROOM / DAY
At the threshold, a high school English teacher who has recently downloaded the Common Core State Standards app reads from her cell phone:
CELL PHONE SCREENSHOT: To become college and career ready, students must grapple with works of exceptional craft and thought whose range extends across genres, cultures, and centuries.

Teacher scrolls down: Along with high-quality contemporary works, these texts should be chosen from among seminal U.S. documents, the classics of American literature, and the timeless dramas of Shakespeare.

Teacher swipes across the screen and enlarges Reading Standard 7: Students must integrate and evaluate content presented in diverse formats and media, including visually and quantitatively, as well as in words.

Teacher enters the Reading Room and approaches the desk.

> Teacher (*in an uncertain tone*): How do I teach students to read literature in words and in diverse formats and media?

CUT TO TITLE SHOT: *The title "Shakespeare" appears in Elizabethan script on a solid background, then "Reading" appears before it in American Typewriter typeface, then the compound adverb "Film First" appears after it.*

> Editor *(in VOICE-OVER)*: Some of the answers will speak from the pages of this book.

1 Reading Still Images

Look here upon this picture, and on this . . .
Hamlet 3.4.63

Let us hold the text of Hamlet's verbal assault upon his mother in one hand and in the other an electronic pad broadcasting an assault of media, and then let us ask our students, who constitute not only a new generation but also perhaps a new breed of learner, to read from both, lowering neither hand to the secondary status of "supplementary." Will the literacy skills required to comprehend twentieth- and twenty-first-century media texts—films, film posters and publicity stills, film trailers, videos, advertisements, websites, newscasts, songs and sound tracks, to name some—transfer to, and in the process transform, our reading of literature and Shakespeare's early modern English text? They will when we expand our understanding of a Shakespeare "edition" to include not only paperbacks and annotated or newly revised editions of his plays but also the great variety of modern forms in which Shakespeare's work is presented. A deep engagement with Shakespeare in the twenty-first century demands the slow reading of Shakespeare in all its iterations. But how do we slow the assault?

Start with stills. Beginning the study of critical viewing with Shakespeare film stills instead of film clips helps students to focus on the elements of visual composition without being overwhelmed by them. Movie posters, for example, are designed to lure viewers to the movie theater, but they can also lure students to the play we are about to read and view in English class. The Internet houses an impressive archive of publicity posters produced for Shakespeare films going back to some of the earliest Hollywood productions.

The Visual Composition

In Chapter 1 of *Seeing and Believing: How to Teach Media Literacy in the English Classroom*, Ellen Krueger and Mary T. Christel pay homage to the authors of a 1968 film textbook long out of print by citing "the five principles of visual composition" (1) outlined by William Kuhns and Robert Stanley and discussing the application of these terms to teaching. The following definitions and bulleted questions are adapted from or inspired by Krueger and Christel's work.

Framing refers to the subject, who or what viewers see, in an image, as well as to the ways in which the camera limits the viewer's field of vision. This can pertain to more than the outer borders of a shot or image; it can, for example, refer to inner frames within a frame such as windows, doorways, arches, or any geometric pattern that focuses attention on a particular space, object, or person (Krueger and Christel 1). On the first day of our study of visual compositions in grade 10 English, I positioned an empty black frame around objects and people in the classroom so that students could immediately see the effects of framing. Then, since we were about to read *Hamlet*, a play that has been filmed "approximately one hundred times" (Jess-Cooke 2), I projected this poster for the 1990 Franco Zeffirelli production onto the whiteboard and asked students:

- Who or what is the subject of this image? What is framed inside the borders of this image? What sort of world is this?
- Inside the outer frame, do you see smaller frames—geometric shapes such as circles, squares, or lines—that draw your attention?

Students saw the subject of this image ranging from the plural to the singular; though they agreed that Hamlet, in the form of Mel Gibson, is the main subject, some students argued that his relationship with the other characters in the image is the real subject. Though this was a prereading activity and few students had prior knowledge of the play, students immediately noted the empty darkness framed within this image and the abrupt vertical line of the sword that divides Mel Gibson's face from Glenn Close's. Though there is no interior architecture in this frame, they noted the horizontal line of troubled faces extending across the image. They seemed curious about the shadowy world boxed inside this frame.

Placement "refers to the position of the camera in relationship to the subject" (Krueger and Christel 1). This can mean the distance and angle of the camera as well as the effect these things have on the viewer's perception of the subject. Though I knew that later in the unit I would distribute a glossary of film terms, we needed to talk quickly about close-up, medium range, and long shots. Drawing a stick figure on the board, I explained that a long shot usually shows the full body, a medium shot is usually from the waist up, and a close-up is usually from the shoulders up. A low-angle camera shot looks up at the subject and tends to make the subject appear larger and perhaps powerful or important, whereas a high-angle camera shot looks down on the subject and can make the subject seem small and sometimes weak or trapped. An eye-level camera shot tends to be natural, or neutral. While director and film scholar Stefan Sharff warns against such oversimplifications of cinematic syntax (32), at this point in our study of camera shots and angles I suggest these readings without insisting on them. Again, using the Zeffirelli *Hamlet* poster, I asked:

- Who, or what, is the subject of this image?
- What is the distance between the camera and the subject—Is it a close-up shot? A medium shot? A long shot? How does the camera distance influence the way you see the subject?
- What is the angle of the camera? High? Low? Eye level? How does the camera angle influence the way you see the subject?

Students agreed that this is a medium shot because Mel Gibson is shown from the waist up, though the people behind him can be seen only from the neck up. They also noted that Gibson is closest to the camera, though Glenn Close seems to be very close too, just behind Gibson and higher.

Some students thought that Gibson and Close must be married or the king and queen in this play, though neither is wearing a crown, and Mel Gibson, as one student pointed out, isn't wearing a wedding band. They counted six people in this image, all arranged very closely—"Too close," one student said—and figured that the people farthest from the camera must be the least important. "If they're close, do they like each other?" I asked. Disagreement ensued; some thought they looked too angry to like each other, but others thought they looked troubled and that they needed to stick together because something was wrong. Students agreed that the camera angle is eye level but thought that only one person, Hamlet, was looking directly at us.

"What effect does that have?" I asked.

"It's like he sees us and he needs to talk to us," one student said.

Subject arrangement is the physical arrangement of people, objects, and background in the frame, which can convey or imply relationships. Arrangement can be, and often is, layered, with some things in the foreground, some in the middle ground, and some in the background. I asked:

- Who or what is in the foreground?
- Is there a middle ground in this image? Who or what is in the middle ground?
- Who or what is farthest from view?
- What does the subject arrangement imply about the relationships in this film?

Though our classroom conversation had already included comments and conjecture about the relationships of the people in this poster, revisiting the image for its layers inspired additional discoveries.

"The sword is the most important thing in the picture because it's in the foreground," one student insisted.

"But Gibson's hands are holding it," another student pointed out.

"Why is the sword upside down? Why does it cover almost half of his face? Why are his hands the object most in the foreground? Why do we see the hands of only one other person in the middle ground? What is this image trying to tell us about the play we're about to read?!" These questions tumbled out of me and over the quizzical faces of my sophomores, and we were struck by how many decisions had to be made to produce this iconic poster.

"And one more thing," I blurted. "Someone thought that the farther the faces got from the foreground—in other words, the faces in the middle ground and the background—the less important the people must be. But are there other ways to think about this?" I wondered.

"Younger to older?" one student offered.

"More powerful to less powerful?" another added.

"Yeah, because Gibson has a sword and he looks really strong, and that guy at the back looks really old and weak," a third student affirmed.

Yes, that guy at the back, I thought, Paul Scofield in the role of the Ghost. Then, as if he could read my thoughts, a student said, "How about more alive to less? Maybe that guy is dead!" I could only smile mysteriously.

Lighting is the intensity of light, or the lack of light, or the contrast between light and shadow in a frame. *Color* is the palette of hues in the image, and as with lighting, its effect can be manipulated through intensity and contrast. In a black-and-white image, the orchestration of grey can be especially significant. Light and color are often used to draw the viewer's eye to a particular place in the frame. Together, light and color can convey the mood of an image. The final question set focused on these two elements of visual composition:

- Where is the light in this image most intense? Who or what is being highlighted?
- What color is most intense in this image?
- What is the effect of darkness or shadows?
- How would you describe the mood of the image, based on its light and color?

Students were most struck by the charge of light that runs from Mel Gibson's clenched hands up through his sword and into the right side of his face. When I asked them what effect the half-light of Gibson's face has on their reading of him, some students thought it made him look more powerful, even dangerous. "Does it make him look less human?" I asked. There was silence, then one student replied, "No, but maybe the sword is more powerful than he is. It's brighter than his hands."

"That's because it's metal and it shines," a student countered.

"Is this a black-and-white photograph?" I asked. "The film isn't shot in black-and-white." There were yeses and nos and the gradual realization that in spite of its limited color palette, this image has a warmth that undercuts Gibson's icy stare and the perceived coldness of the metal shaft in his hands.

"It's black and goldish," a student declared. Though I had cast my eyes upon this image countless times since first seeing it in 1990, not until this class discussion did I really see that this image speaks in the warm, sepia dialect of early modern photography. I found myself thinking of Claudius's question to Hamlet in 1.2, "How is it that the clouds still hang on you?" and Hamlet's enigmatic reply, "Not so, my lord, I am too much i' th' sun."

"Based on the colors and the light, what word would you use to describe the mood of this image?" I asked.

"Dark."

"But hopeful."

"Tense."

"All mixed up." That one caught me by surprise.

"What do you mean? Isn't this a simple color palette? Isn't this light and dark, angels and demons, good and evil?" I prodded them, gently mocking the adolescent tendency to divide the literary world into two-dimensional heroes and villains.

"These might all be good people, but they all have shadows. Maybe that symbolizes something," a young woman said. I wanted to hug her but instead I just smiled. They were almost ready to begin reading *Hamlet*.

After this introduction and whole-group discussion of a single film poster for the play we were about to read (see Handout 1.1 for the set of bulleted questions; handouts are in the appendix), I distributed color prints of two other *Hamlet* film posters (see Figure 1.1) and challenged students to read these new images in small groups and discuss the ways in which the posters are constructed from the raw material of framing, placement, subject arrangement, lighting, and color.

To support students' understanding of the complexity of visual composing and to guide their discussion, I created Handout 1.2 so that it relates each principle to a job at a construction site, defines each element, and includes the bulleted questions that guided our whole-group analysis of the Zeffirelli poster. Because I wrote these questions with the three images before me, as well as with posters of other films, Handouts 1.1 and 1.2 can be used with almost any film poster or publicity still.

In the spirit of *not* judging a book by its cover, colleague Tim Alperen extended this activity in his grade 9 English classroom to the reading of *Othello* book covers in a variety of print editions. The commentary for each image is Alperen's:

Hamlet. 1990. 135 minutes. Directed by Franco Zeffirelli. Mel Gibson as Hamlet.	*Hamlet*. 1996. 242 minutes. Directed by Kenneth Branagh. Branagh as Hamlet.	*Hamlet*. 2000. 123 minutes. Directed by Michael Almereyda. Ethan Hawke as Hamlet.

Figure 1.1. Posters for three different film versions of *Hamlet*.

The **Dover Edition** (this is the edition students will read from) is a painting depicting the perverse consummation of Othello's relationship with Desdemona, either after or during her death. This Othello is clearly dark skinned, and the expression on his face is enigmatic, open to a range of interpretations from "guilty" to "remorseful" to "deceptive." In the painting, Othello holds a pillow, but prior to reading the play, kids don't really know what to make of it, so this is worth revisiting when we encounter the "smothering," as there are, indeed, textual variants governing the stage directions here, and this image is arguably an editorial emendation that persists somewhere between the choice of cover and text of this edition.

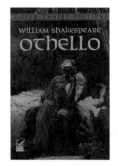

The **Arden Edition** simply shows a white handkerchief in mid flight against a black backdrop, my personal favorite because of its ambiguity. Postreading *Othello*, it's pretty clear that it is a hanky, but prior to experiencing the play it can actually be difficult to discern what it is or what it signifies. I have seen kids screw their faces up in consternation and bewilderment trying to make sense of it.

The **No Fear Edition**, which, for the record, I do not use but some kids do bring to class, does work in our lesson. The image on the cover is ambiguous: sketches of the barest of outlines of two faces—both with green eyes, which is actually a nice touch, you have to admit. The fact that there are two faces could be evocative of Janus, but I do not provoke thoughts in any direction, especially at this point when we are first getting started on the text; ideas of what the images imply *after* reading the text are compared to our first readings of the book covers—this holds for all editions.

The **Folger Edition** is another really good one, especially to the extent that it doesn't lead the jury, if you will, anywhere. It's a mass of color, a textured swath of reddish blackish something! Students have no idea whether it is an extreme close-up of a detail or brushstroke from a painting—it could be a bloodstain seen through a microscope. When forced to guess at the intentions of this visual composition other than intentional ambiguity or even misdirection, some students might suggest passion overriding reason.

The **Norton Critical Edition** is adorned with a portrait of the Moorish ambassador to Queen Elizabeth in 1600. Given the nature of the Norton edition, it makes sense for them to opt for a more empirical consideration of the cover image. Whether William Shakespeare actually saw this man in London, as some scholars wishfully wonder, the image is a fascinating study in cultural and psychological messages.

The obvious summarizer to an introductory lesson on reading visual compositions is to ask students to make predictions about the literary elements of the play they are about to read—the characters, conflict, mood, and themes—based on the images they practiced reading in the movie posters. In the grade 10 *Hamlet* classroom, the Zeffirelli poster helped students to predict that there will be action, conflict, murder, and death in the play. "There will be royal problems," Jeanette and Diego predicted based on the Branagh poster. "Someone gets married and Hamlet isn't happy about it."

The Almereyda poster inspired the most intense conjecture. Some students thought that by placing his hands on top of his head, Hawke's Hamlet, unlike Gibson's, "is not in control of the action," or that "he will go through a series of actions that he made up in his head." Jimmy and Soun predicted that this Hamlet "puts his hands on his head to symbolize that his mind is more powerful than his hands."

On this day I discovered almost by accident that teaching students to read different film posters of the same play establishes what Shakespeare scholar Jonathan Bate calls "the first law" of Shakespeare, which is that "truth is not singular" (327). Seeing words and images in duplicate and triplicate encourages students of all ability levels to play with the possibilities of text.

The Commercial Composition

A film poster is an advertisement for a commercial product as well as an artistic one, and the lesson narrated in this chapter on the principles of visual composition can and should be extended to include the ways in which images are packaged to appeal to consumers and to elicit a response. So the next day I asked students to search online for posters of popular teen films and, using Handout 1.2 as a guide, to identify the elements of visual composition. Students clustered in small groups around computers in the library media center and engaged in exuberant chatter as posters of teen films flickered across the screens. Javier even found a poster for a 1998 action movie called *Thundercats* that appears to be modeled on the 1990 Zeffirelli *Hamlet* poster.

As an extension of what they were learning about reading visual compositions, I wanted students to link the visual elements—framing, placement, subject arrangement, lighting and color—to a poster's message and commercial appeal. So after each group had settled on a single poster and filled Handout 1.2 with their notes, I projected these summary questions on the whiteboard:

- What do you know about the writer, the director, or the producer of the film?
- What message does the poster send about the film?
- Who is the target audience for the poster and the film? How do you know?
- Do you find the poster appealing? Why?

But as I checked in with students, none knew anything about the writers, directors, or producers of their favorite films, and all assumed that they themselves were the target audience. When I asked them for visual evidence of the posters' messages and appeals, they pointed to the most obvious elements of the posters, such as the titles, the slogans, the movie stars, and the props.

Though the day before beginning a play by William Shakespeare might not be the best time to launch a study of the messages and values implicit in commercial images, I hoped that our closing discussion would set the stage for such a future lesson. So we bravely returned to the three *Hamlet* posters to reread them now not as visual compositions but as advertisements for a product. The discussion confirmed that while students were gaining an understanding of visual literacy, their knowledge of media literacy was limited.

Borrowing a graphic organizer from the grade 11 Advanced Placement English Language and Composition course as a visual anchor for our summary discussion, I projected the rhetorical triangle on the whiteboard (see Figure 1.2). This was the first (but not the last) time my sophomores would work with the triangle. When I asked them what commercial message each poster sends about *Hamlet*, they reverted to observations made the day before about the literary messages regarding characters, conflict, imagery, and themes.

"Think of the word *message* as an opinion or claim," I said. "What claim does the Zeffirelli poster make about *Hamlet*?" Silence ensued, so I rephrased. "Does this poster say, 'I don't care what you've been told about Shakespeare. This flick is macho and action-packed!'?" Silence.

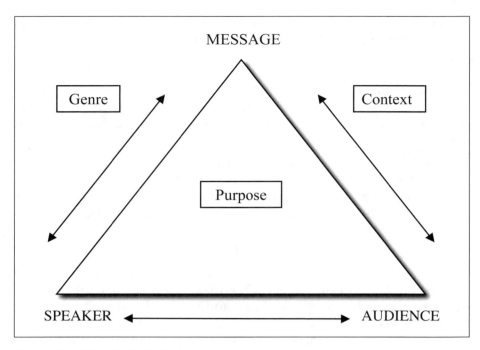

Figure 1.2. The rhetorical triangle.

"Does the Almereyda poster say, 'So what if Shakespeare's been dead for 400 years. This *Hamlet* is high-tech!'?" Silence.

"Okay, what type of film does the Branagh poster present *Hamlet* as? What genre?" The rest was silence.

"Rhetoric," write Hephzibah Roskelly and David Jolliffe, "is the art that humans use to process all the messages we send and receive" (2). Because the primary focus of my course at this time was to prepare students to read the literary message of *Hamlet*, tomorrow we would move beyond visual compositions into the wild and whirling world of words. But I knew that I would need to explore more fully with all of my students the rhetorical structures and strategies employed by poets, princes, and producers.

2 Reading Commercial Images

Who chooseth me shall gain what many men desire. . . .
Who chooseth me shall get as much as he deserves. . . .
Who chooseth me must give and hazard all he hath.

The Merchant of Venice 2.7.5–12

Students know that reading Shakespeare requires risk; in fact, risk is one of the things that draws them to the plays. But when we engage students in an examination of what Kenneth S. Rothwell calls "the most cash-driven art form in history" and the ways in which Shakespeare is "commodified" (3), they enter the marketplace like the fortune-seekers in *The Merchant of Venice*, reading the messages on the gold, silver, and lead caskets, and consider the challenge of translating Shakespeare's artistic and commercial risk into profit.

Using posters, publicity stills, and film trailers, this chapter merges the concepts of visual and commercial compositions introduced in Chapter 1 into a unit of study that explores the commercialization of Shakespeare's text in the consumer age. Though they may enter the conversation as passive visual consumers, students will exit it with the perspective of producers who must give and hazard all they have to bring Shakespeare into the modern film marketplace.

Posters, Publicity Stills, and Commercial Art

Though most years we end the Shakespeare course with *The Tempest*—"I shall miss thee; / But yet thou shalt have freedom. . . ." (5.1.105–6)—in the fall of 2010, when I learned that a new film production of *The Tempest* was scheduled for release in December, I shuffled the course syllabus and brought Shakespeare's final play forward. Recalling the work begun in the previous year with sophomores reading *Hamlet*, I hoped that the media hype surrounding this new release would generate fresh material for a fuller examination of the methods by which artists and marketers collaborate to attract new audiences to a four-hundred-year-old script.

Just as I began a year ago with the iconic 1990 *Hamlet* film poster and a different group of students, I projected this 2010 poster for *The Tempest* onto the SMART Board and distributed Handout 1.1 to guide our

opening discussion. Students immediately commented on the three faces within the three interior frames and the three dancing figures in the middle frame. (Since we had not begun reading the play, students were unaware of director Julie Taymor's decision to recast Prospero as Prospera in the person of Helen Mirren.) They observed that the borders between each frame are compromised by flying debris and flames. Unlike the 1990 Zeffirelli poster with its famous faces in the foreground, students could not name any of the actors in this poster but most said their attention was drawn to the middle frame because that face seems more "sympathetic" and is the only face on the left side looking to the right. This observation stunned me into remembering that a left-to-right visual code reinforces the way we read both text and film, and is therefore "sanctified as the right way" (Cartmell 6) by Western filmmakers; more often than not, the so-called good guys move from left of frame to right. Students were fascinated by the complexity of this poster, and our whole-group analysis elicited genuine interest in the brave new world of a play and a film we had not yet read.

Next I divided students into small groups and gave each group a different print of a publicity still from a collection published at the

film's promotional website, along with sticky notes to attach comments to their images. Though I had not foreseen this, students seemed to transfer their first impressions of the poster, a single composition carefully divided, to their visual analyses of the stills. Still using Handout 1.1 as a guide, students consistently made observations about a world that is divided and threatening. Lillian, Marissa, and Aaron noted that this image conveys conflict on two levels—the rocky terrain in the foreground and the ocean in the background reinforce the physical arrangement of natural elements and characters posed in aggressive opposition to each other. Even their examination of light and color reinforces this: "Most light," one sticky note reads, "is on the girls and the water; less light is on the man and the land. The color of his costume and his skin suggests that he is associated with the land." Another note reads, "The framing is hostile—conflict between cultures— the lines are horizontal but the people divide vertically at the left and right of the frame."

In reading a different still, another group noted the natural division between land and sky, as well as the sky divided by clouds. They noted

a circle on the ground as an inner frame and wondered if it were some sort of "fighting ring" since the long shot places a man in the foreground "sizing up" the next most important figure, the weaponless woman. Because the "old guy" in the back left doesn't have a weapon either, they read this arrangement of characters as two opposing sides, with the more vulnerable and defensive group on the left side of the frame and the more threatening and aggressive group on the right. Still, in their examination of color, these students noticed that "they dress similarly so they must all come from the same background. . . . They all look noble."

Anyone familiar with *The Tempest* will be struck, as I was, by the dual insight students gained from this activity as both a graphic reading and literary prereading exercise. Before venturing into the literary and theatrical world of *The Tempest*, we would spend the next day reading commercial images to study the tools of visual composition employed by commercial artists—framing, placement, subject arrangement, lighting, and color—to appeal to modern viewers.

Posters, Publicity Stills, and Artistic Commerce

Producing a film can cost millions of dollars; in the 1990s, when Shakespeare on film enjoyed a renaissance with the production of twenty major films based on Shakespeare's plays, the budgets ran from less than $1 million to almost $20 million (Crowl 81). Producing a film adaptation of a play by William Shakespeare is especially risky in the American pop culture market. The bigger the budget, the more pressure the producer feels to appeal to a wider audience. How this pressure influences the product—a twenty-first-century film production of *Hamlet* or *Othello*, for example—is a fascinating study in artistic and commercial chemistry.

"Adaptation," explains Carolyn Jess-Cooke, author of *Shakespeare on Film*, "is a blanket term for the process by which a text is visualized on screen" (34). There seems to be no agreed-upon taxonomy among scholars for classifying all the different types of films inspired by Shakespeare, but the term most often used for a film that is spoken in Shakespeare's language and set in a historical period other than the one in which the film is produced is an adaptation: Taymor's 2010 production of *The Tempest* falls into this category. Cultural adaptations are contemporary updates of a play, spoken in Shakespeare's language but translated into modern culture by way of a rich and strange array of visual and auditory codes from modern life. Learning that a cultural adaptation of *Coriolanus*, set not in ancient Rome but in a twenty-first-century war zone, was currently in production, I decided to bookend the film poster of Taymor's adaptation with two film posters of cultural adaptations, Baz Luhrmann's 1996 *William Shakespeare's Romeo+Juliet* and Ralph Fiennes's 2011 *Coriolanus* (see Figure 2.1).

During a conversation with Allison Giordano Casper, a colleague who teaches *Othello* to ninth graders at the same time I teach *Hamlet* to sophomores, we drew upon our shared experience teaching Advanced Placement English Language and Composition, a course that focuses on the study of rhetoric. Adapting the rhetorical triangle to the context of Shakespeare on film, we modified the speaker-message-audience triangle diagrammed in Chapter 1 by using the concrete nouns of commercialism (see Figure 2.2). When students consider the interconnected points of this triangle, they begin to see Shakespeare on film as both an artistic and a commercial risk.

A fundamental shift in perspective from publicity stills and posters as commercial art to stills and posters as artistic commerce began at the end of the lesson when I projected this image and asked students to respond to the prompt: "How does the **producer** of each poster package

William Shakespeare's Romeo + Juliet. Directed by Baz Luhrmann. 1996.	The Tempest. Directed by Julie Taymor. 2010.	Coriolanus. Directed by Ralph Fiennes. 2011.

Figure 2.1. Movie posters of cultural adaptations of Shakespeare plays.

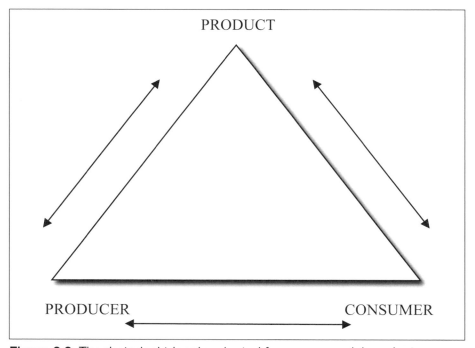

Figure 2.2. The rhetorical triangle adapted for a commercial product.

Shakespeare as a commercial **product** with popular appeal to a wide range of **consumers**?" Marissa commented that everyone knows *Romeo and Juliet* is a love story, but Luhrmann's poster "does some arithmetic with Shakespeare's formula, substituting his characters with current actors and his words with symbols, color, and images." She noted the plus sign in the title, the twelve guns pointed in two directions, the orange sky, the flaming heart, and the paradoxical quote, "My only love sprung from my only hate." In gazing intently at each of the first two posters, a roomful of young adults saw reflections of an audience that included them as well as others: "teenagers, adults, men, women, people who don't read Shakespeare." But the *Coriolanus* poster seemed to have a more limited appeal. "This poster says *Coriolanus* is for men," Taylor stated. "Simple men." When I laughed and objected that this college-educated woman can't wait to see it, she explained, "Well, you're different, Ms. Dakin, you're an English teacher!"

In the closing minutes of class, we were stumbling into what David Bordwell calls "maximal design" (qtd. in Cook 20), or the attempt by Shakespeare film producers to appeal to a wide audience that includes viewers who don't read Shakespeare as well as those who do, but also more specialized subgroups whose interests and expertise must be appealed to if the film is to earn artistic as well as commercial success: "Shakespeare scholars, cineastes and film scholars, fellow filmmakers, auteurists who follow the director's career, and numerous other subgroups" (Cook 20)—including, as Taylor put it, English teachers.

Because one of my main purposes in the Shakespeare class is to explore with students the infinite ways in which Shakespeare can be transmediated from literary script to film, our lesson ended here, with much lively discussion. Because our primary purpose in the English language and composition course is to explore the myriad messages we send and receive, my colleague's lesson began where I had left off. Before projecting the commercial triangle (see Figure 2.3) and the three Shakespeare film posters, Casper asked her students to think about how films are marketed to them. The first question generated a list of elements that appeal to a teen audience; the second question identified three of the most effective strategies (formatted in **bold**):

> What factors influence what films you watch? Which factors are most influential?
>
> - Director
> - Special effects/3D
> - Time of year of the film release

- Genre
- Actors/star quality
- **Popularity/"buzz"**
- Setting of the film
- Reviews/recommendations
- Plot/narrative content
- **Posters—theater, billboards, magazines**
- **Trailers—websites, previews in theaters, commercials**

Though actors, special effects, even plot might contribute to the "buzz," Casper's students unanimously agreed that the single most effective factor in getting them inside a movie theater is *buzz*, defined at the *Urban Dictionary* ("Buzz") as "anything that generates excitement, hype, cool gossip." Buzz is spoken, tweeted, texted, YouTubed hype.

Not knowing in advance the extent to which her students would recognize posters as important factors in the marketing of a film, Casper

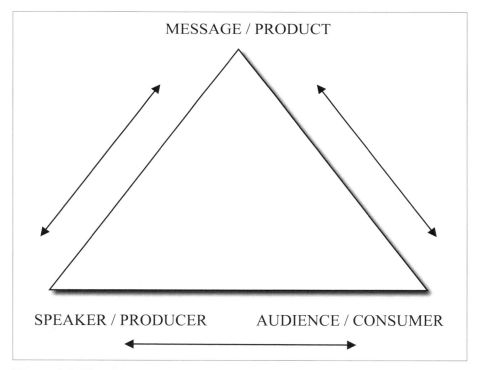

Figure 2.3. The commercial triangle.

projected the familiar rhetorical triangle, added the concrete nouns of commercialism, and explained that the focus of their analysis today would be three Shakespeare film posters. Viewing one poster at a time, Casper's students would discuss two questions:

> How does the **producer** attempt to package Shakespeare as a commercial film **product**? What **message** does the poster send?

> Who is the intended **audience/consumer** for the product? (Gender, age group, education level, etc.) How is this reflected in the image?

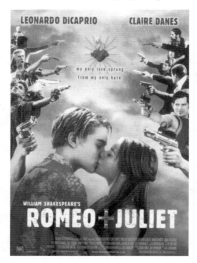

If students accustomed to reading rhetorical nonfiction, news photos, and political cartoons seemed suddenly taken aback, the first poster brought them forward. The bright colors, the well-known actors, the familiar title, the image of the sacred heart of Jesus familiar to some students, the act of kissing at gunpoint, and the message of love in a violent world—students commented on these elements as having an immediate commercial appeal to a teenage audience drawn to films about rebellious love. Though indecipherable on the poster, one of the countless brilliant cultural updates that Luhrmann makes to Shakespeare's text can be read in the screenplay when Benvolio cries, "Put up your swords!" and "A SUPER MACRO SLAM ZOOM along the barrel of Benvolio's gun" reveals "the engraved gun type: 'Sword 9mm series S'" (Pearce and Luhrmann 7).

Students accustomed to analyzing the rhetorical structure of an argument recognized in the triple frames of *The Tempest* poster a commercial appeal to a wide range of audiences. The diversity of gender, age, race, and genre evident in each frame, the ambiguous relationships between each group, and the implied struggle for power and survival dramatized throughout the poster were seen as deliberate appeals to viewers who like fantasy, action, and adventure, but also to older or more educated viewers who appreciate seeing women and minorities in roles of power. Students even

noted that this poster utilizes the natural elements of fire, earth, sky, and wind in its design to explain the title visually, thus encouraging a non-Shakespeare-reading audience to believe that the movie will help them understand Shakespeare's words through images and action.

Students found the *Coriolanus* poster to be almost deceptive advertising in that, of all the posters, it most successfully minimizes Shakespeare. To begin with, they reasoned that most American audiences have never heard of *Coriolanus* and have no idea that Shakespeare wrote it, and this poster does nothing to change that; this in itself ensures a wider audience appeal! Second, the contemporary images appeal directly to a modern audience drawn to films about violence and war. Casper's students considered the outline of a gun the most prominent design feature, but they also identified the eye-level gaze of a man, the finger on the trigger, the bullet holes in concrete, the grey color scheme and the red letters, the city at the bottom of the frame—the set of modern violence and the backdrop of media news reports—and the ominous quote "Nature teaches beasts to know their friends" as appeals to a male  audience, from young to middle-aged, though the fact that two famous actors star in the film and one of them is considered a sex symbol might attract a female audience.

"The iron rule of profit or perish," observes Rothwell, has "forced the Shakespeare director into an inevitable synergy with popular culture" (3). From the box office to the twenty-first-century classroom, engaging young people in a critical analysis of the commercial appeals embedded in Shakespeare film posters and publicity stills adds a new scaffold to the construction of understanding their world. Once students see the infrastructure of an argument and hear the transmissions that fly along the circuitry of sender-message-receiver, they are better equipped to succeed in a world where seeing is *not* believing; seeing is understanding.

The Art and Craft of Trailers

Film trailers, a commercial art form for the past one hundred years, were named in the days of silent film because they were shown *after* the feature film instead of before it, as now. It didn't take long for the industry to realize that people were walking out of movie houses at the very time they could be persuaded to return. Today, if a film is scheduled to start at 7:00 p.m., it's common to watch fifteen minutes or more of film trailers before the film we paid to see actually begins. Guidelines imposed by the Motion Picture Association of America (MPAA) require that trailers produced for viewing in movie theaters sell a film in two and a half minutes or less (televised trailers are usually shorter; online trailers can exceed this time frame), which means that modern trailers must appeal to a wide audience in ways that are both more obvious and more subtle than their still-image cousins.

In the library of film history and scholarship, little has been published on the genre of film trailers. But from hours of viewing and talking about Shakespeare film trailers at home, in school, and with colleagues, and from scattered references in film texts and continuously updated online sources such as Wikipedia, we can craft a work-in-progress that challenges our students and ourselves to analyze the pop culture synergy that ignites the Shakespeare film trailer.

Composed from the *dailies*, defined in *The Complete Film Production Handbook* as "footage that's been shot[,] . . . processed[,] . . . and printed . . . for viewing the next day" (Honthaner 510), and sometimes from "special shoot" footage that will never appear in the film, trailers are produced before the film itself has undergone final edits and well before the film's sound track has been composed. This scenario provides film trailer producers, editors, and sound engineers with a creative freedom that almost equals that of modern Shakespeare film producers.

Freelance film and television editor Ken Yankee explains that scenes included in a trailer are condensed into "short, concise bites" and assembled into a "rough cut" that is not necessarily the order in which the full scenes will appear in the film. Editing bites into a two-and-a-half-minute trailer that tells enough to sell a film almost always requires some use of printed text—titles and intertitles—and may require voice-over narration, though this method is used less frequently now than in the past. Sound design, however, has become increasingly sophisticated in trailers, with a complex layering of sound effects, music, music stops, music changes, and snippets of dialogue (Yankee).

The overall structure of a trailer usually follows the classic Hollywood three-act model for screenwriting formulated in 1979 by Syd Fields (Thompson 22), with some modifications to the third act:

First Act: Major problems are introduced.

Second Act: Problems intensify toward a seemingly irresolvable climax.

Third Act: Problems are solved.

By the time I had prepared a lesson on reading the 2010 film trailer for *The Tempest*, students had read to the end of act 3 in the play, but this was an advantage in that trailers can't spoil the final outcome of the film they entice viewers to see, so they generally consist of a sequence of rapid scenes taken from the beginning and middle of the film story. A Wikipedia article on the topic of film promotion and trailers notes that the third act of a modern trailer usually shifts to some combination of a dramatic visual montage,[1] emotionally charged signature music, and a cast run ("Trailer [film]"). Because of time constraints, students would not be producing their own trailer for *The Tempest*, but we would begin by brainstorming for such a challenge.

Unlike trailers produced before the 1960s, with their stock reliance on adjectives such as *Colossal!* and *Stupendous!*, the 2010 *Tempest* trailer scatters a series of abstract nouns across frames. From this device, I constructed a first step in the process of understanding how a trailer producer might begin to select from the hours of raw footage a collection of key images that conveys the problems in a Shakespeare film: I asked students to name the major conflicts in Shakespeare's play using abstract nouns. They responded with these nouns in this order:

POWER	ART	LOYALTY
AUTHORITY	MAGIC	RACISM
REVENGE	DECEPTION	TIME
TRUST	KNOWLEDGE	GREED
IGNORANCE	BETRAYAL	FREEDOM
LOVE	FORGIVENESS	

Working in small production teams, students selected from our list only the abstract nouns that they believed name the most profound problems in this play. With books in hand, students scanned the first three acts of the play looking for events and key lines that dramatically convey the abstract nouns they had chosen. Finally, each team arranged their collection of "clips" or "bites" along a simple timeline using a fishbone graphic organizer and in the process assembled the raw materials of a "rough cut" that introduces new or struggling readers to this play and builds toward a troubling climax in act 3. Working in a team of three students who agreed that *The Tempest* is driven by issues of power, revenge, and greed, student Kate Ferrante constructed the section of her team's graphic organizer seen in Figure 2.4.

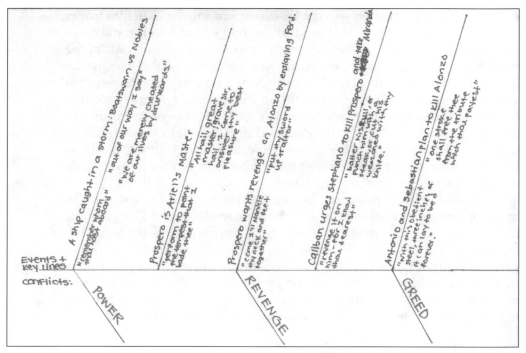

Figure 2.4. Student team's graphic organizer for *The Tempest* incorporating the themes of power, revenge, and greed.

On the second day, after we shared ideas about the major problems and key scenes or lines that convey those problems, I displayed my film trailer adaptation of the three-act model for screenwriting:

The Structure of a Film Trailer

Film trailers can be divided into a **beginning, middle**, and **end** using this formula:

> **Act 1** of the trailer establishes the major conflicts of the film.
>
> **Act 2** of the trailer drives the conflicts toward a climax.
>
> **Act 3** of the trailer concludes with emotionally charged signature music (this might be popular music familiar to the audience or a symphonic composition) and a dramatic visual montage.

I asked students to imagine that they have less than three minutes to sell *The Tempest* to a modern film audience and then to think about the timelines they had constructed as the raw footage of a film trailer for the play.

What abstract nouns would guide their vision of the major problems in this play? What actions and words from the play, combined with images and sounds, would they use? After distributing a simple preproduction storyboard template, I projected the challenge: "Storyboard a three-act movie trailer for *The Tempest*!" Figure 2.5 is one example of a first-draft trailer storyboard, composed by student Charlie Wongwajarachot.

After sharing their ideas as film trailer producers by projecting their storyboards using the document reader, the students were ready to analyze what a team of professionals had done with the same challenge. Projecting the 2010 *The Tempest* film trailer from the film's publicity website onto the SMART Board, we began our first viewing as a holistic introduction to a complex, rapid-fire commercial composition.

Wow. Please pardon the interjection, but this was the immediate whole-group reaction to the first viewing of the trailer. "You want us to analyze that?" was the second. Handout 2.1[2] is my response.

The brevity of a film trailer makes multiple viewings a convenient necessity. At the end of the third viewing, when students were just beginning to agree on a beginning, middle, and end for the *Tempest* trailer, Guil and Jordan, both student musicians in our school's Rock Ensemble, requested that we conduct a fourth "viewing" minus the video. They wanted the rest of us to hear what they thought they heard—a beginning, middle, and end punctuated by sound effects, music changes, and dialogue. Through a dynamic combination of viewing and listening, students finally agreed on the three-part structural framework of this trailer.

From this whole-group analysis, students broke into smaller teams to focus on the words, the sound track, and the cast run. After sharing their observations with the whole group, we ended with a discussion of the commercial triangle and the extent to which this trailer would entice an audience into a movie theater. "We're sold!" Juliana proclaimed. "When is the field trip?" These two lessons, conducted midway in our reading of *The Tempest*, contributed not only to my students' enthusiasm for this play but also to our growing sense of Shakespeare as an artistic and commercial force in their lives.

Suspecting that high school students who choose the Shakespeare elective in their junior or senior year are already sold on Shakespeare, I wondered about the practicality of spending one or two class periods in a regular English classroom learning to analyze the film trailer for a Shakespeare play that students will not read. Would students reject such an exercise as irrelevant or too difficult? Just as she had countless times in the past, English department colleague Althea Terenzi eagerly took up the challenge with her seniors, who several months later would read

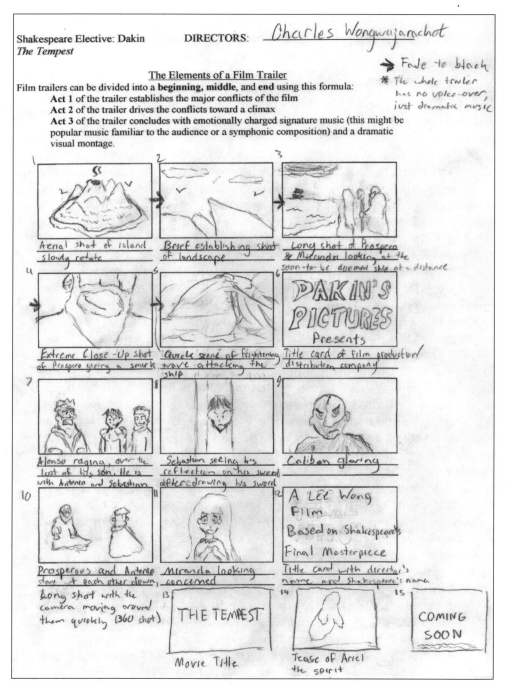

Figure 2.5. Student storyboard of a movie trailer for *The Tempest*.

not from *The Tempest* but from *A Midsummer Night's Dream*. "Of course," Terenzi told me after her students had engaged in a lively examination of the material, "now they are asking to please read *Tempest* instead." Terenzi's work convinced me that, with minor modifications, learning to read a Shakespeare film trailer will help all our students to more fully understand both words in the term *pop culture*.

Because her students were completely unfamiliar with *The Tempest*, Terenzi began with the trailer, prefacing the first viewing with simple instructions. Since every narrative develops a problem, Terenzi told her students to jot down what they think the conflicts in this story are, using abstract nouns. Her students copied down the words that appear in the trailer—*sorcery, passion, stupidity, revenge*—but they also added *treachery, betrayal, greed, ownership,* and *war*.

For the second viewing, students needed to make the abstract concrete by keeping notes on how these conflicts are established in the trailer using images, sound, and dialogue. Students noted the "fire stick" as a symbol for sorcery, Russell Brand's strange wardrobe as an image of stupidity, the young lovers as embodying passion, and the image of two men drawing swords on a sleeping brother as an act of treachery. They considered the dramatic delivery of the line "This island's mine" as a statement of ownership, power, and greed and the "fire dogs and creepy bird-guy" as instruments of revenge.

Before the third viewing, Terenzi distributed the three-tiered *Tempest* film poster and prepared students to identify the three-act structure of the trailer, but her students immediately voiced concerns that this activity would be too difficult because the whole trailer is so fast-paced and intense. Together they discussed the best way to chunk a trailer. "Do you just want to watch the whole trailer and take notes as you watch," Terenzi asked, "or signal me to pause the trailer at the end of a chunk while you take notes?" Students decided there might be too much disagreement about the chunks, and that they'd rather take notes on their own and then compare.

But after the third viewing, Terenzi's students came to an easy consensus about the beginning, middle, and end of this trailer. The climax, they agreed, begins when the word *revenge* appears and the image of the sharp needle or feather dropping into a beaker explodes. They characterized the "fire dogs," the "bird-man," and the line "I have made you mad" as constituting the most intense, climactic segment of the trailer. Unlike my students, who knew from their reading of the play that Miranda and Ferdinand "at the first sight . . . have changed eyes" in act 1, scene 2, a few students in Terenzi's class commented that the introduction of the lovers, with its shift in music, had tricked them into thinking the climax had already passed, when instead the intensity rebuilds immediately afterward. They agreed that the conclusion begins with the Sigur Ros song "Saeglopur," just as the cast run and credits come up.

For their fourth viewing, students listened to the trailer without seeing it and took notes. Only now did they begin to hear the layers of sound and the connections between sound change and image sequence. They noted repeated buildups of music, and then crashing sounds and explosions. They said they could hear when a new word appears onscreen because the music changes, a connection they hadn't noticed while viewing. They also said they could hear the climax coming without seeing any images because "a bass drum builds up." The trailer, they noted, is bookended by Prospera speaking, and the music at the conclusion is "empowering, like everything will be okay, but in some sad or nostalgic way." The timing and vocal tone of Prospera's last line made it seem "very important or thematic."

As if she had foreseen that her students would wonder about the last line in the trailer, "We are such stuff / As dreams are made on, and our little life / Is rounded with a sleep" (4.1.173–75), Terenzi was prepared: she projected the text of Prospero's most famous sentence and students discussed the lines. "So the fire dogs, the bird-man, the sinking ship, were all just in their heads? Is all of life an illusion? Is it saying life is short, like a nap? Is it saying our life *is* our dreams?" Her students questioned, in a discussion that lasted almost five minutes. Finally, they looked at these lines in the full context of the speech "Our revels now are ended . . ." and students were better able to understand the quote and to discuss the film trailer in light of this famous speech from the play.

At some point in our exploration of commercial art and popular culture, we come full circle. After repeated viewings of a collection of Shakespeare publicity stills, posters, and film trailers, the questions students raise are among the questions that William Shakespeare himself asks repeatedly throughout the plays.

Our students inhabit a visual world, yet they struggle to see the bones of composition and to read the messages embedded in text, images, film, and commercials. If "[e]verything's an argument" (Lunsford, Ruszkiewicz, and Walters), the "everything" of the English classroom is exponentially greater now—the poet appeals, the speaker debates, the artist interprets, the musician arranges, the photographer frames, and the filmmaker transmediates the business of life into images and sound.

3 Recognizing the Three Faces of Film

Stay, illusion!
If thou hast any sound or use of voice,
Speak to me.

Hamlet 1.1.139–41

There are so many ways to tell a story, but with Shakespeare the trinity of telling is literary, theatrical, and cinematic, in roughly that order. We begin (even if we are actors in preproduction) with Shakespeare on the page but soon learn (even if we are teachers and students in an English classroom) that his words must be made flesh. We add modern tools to the storyteller's art, and *cinematography*, which literally means "writing in movement" (Jess-Cooke 65), completes the circuit of Shakespeare's triangle, as depicted in Figure 3.1.

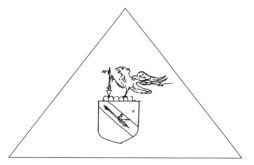

Literary: Characters, setting, conflict, language, tone, point of view, mood, symbols, purpose, message, theme, audience/reader

Theatrical: Actors, acting, (voice, facial expression, gesture, movement), costumes, makeup, sets, props, lights, sound, audience

Cinematic: Cameras (shots, angles, framing, focus, movement), editing, realistic locations and sets, lighting, sound (vocal, environmental, musical, silent), special effects, titles, and intertitles, animation, audience/viewer

Figure 3.1. Shakespeare's triangle.

This chapter builds on the fundamental concepts of composing still images as it introduces students to the process of actively reading film clips. It establishes an approach to critical viewing that begins with the most familiar elements of storytelling, the literary and theatrical, and works toward the least familiar, the cinematic. The classroom scenario in which this chapter is grounded is the most common one—students are reading Shakespeare's play word first, but they are also learning to read images and film. The critical viewing strategies outlined in this and the next two chapters provide a foundation for reading Shakespeare with film or on film that informs every teaching scenario.

Triangulating the Text

With a question—"What are your ten favorite movies?"—Alan B. Teasley and Ann Wilder, authors of *Reel Conversations*, begin the process of teaching students in the English classroom to see film as more than a retelling of a literary story and as an art form in its own right (15). On a winter day in 2009, with a set of questions inspired by the work of Teasley and Wilder and John Golden, the juniors and seniors in my Shakespeare elective temporarily put aside our reading of *King Lear* to begin to learn how to read *Lear* on film. In March 2009, PBS planned to release a new production of *Lear* directed by Trevor Nunn and starring Ian McKellan, and my students and I had been invited to participate in a *King Lear* Web seminar sponsored by PBS and the Folger Shakespeare Library. Since that time, with each succeeding group of students, not only in the Shakespeare elective but in every English course that I teach as well, I have returned to this lesson as a necessary extension of the principles of visual literacy outlined in Chapter 1 and as a foundational introduction to film and media literacy.

With their lists of Top Ten Movies before them, I asked students why they liked these films. Their answers had all to do with the actors or the story and nothing to do with cinematography. Now was the time to introduce them to the three faces of film: literary, theatrical, and cinematic (Teasley and Wilder 15–24). Characters, setting, conflict and action, language, mood, tone, symbols, theme—these are literary elements that films and literature share. So I asked them to meet in small groups to discuss the literary elements of their favorite film, guided by this question set that I modified from Teasley and Wilder:

Who are the <u>characters </u>in the film?
What is the film's <u>setting</u>?

What happens? Briefly summarize the <u>plot</u>.

How "literary" is the <u>dialogue</u>? How significant is the <u>language</u>?

What is the vocal <u>tone</u> of the dialogue?

From whose <u>point of view</u> is the story told?

Who is the film's intended <u>audience</u>?

What is the <u>mood</u> of the film?

What objects in the film function as <u>symbols</u>?

What is the film's <u>purpose</u>, beyond entertainment?

What issues and ideas seem important? What are the <u>themes </u>of the film?

Though our discussion of film adaptations of literature would eventually focus on Shakespeare's plays, none of my students' top ten movies included a Shakespeare film or a film adapted from any literary classic. Still, their conversations were rich and animated, and as I listened in on the groups, I was struck by the students' ability to see film's literary face.

The second set of questions focuses students' gaze on the progression of a text from page to stage. Actors, costumes, makeup, sets—these are the theatrical aspects of film that I worked into the second question set:

How do the <u>actors</u> interpret the characters they play?

How do the <u>costumes</u> and <u>makeup</u> reinforce the acting?

Describe the main <u>sets</u> and the most interesting <u>props</u>.

Do <u>lighting</u> and <u>color</u> contribute to the drama? How?

Do <u>sound</u> and/or <u>silence</u> contribute to the drama? How?

Students had much to say about the actors, costumes, sets, and props, but their recall of the subtler elements of lighting, color, and sound was limited. After they discussed the literary and theatrical aspects of their favorite films, I asked another question: "How are movies different from books and plays?" There was an odd silence, as though somehow they had never considered this question. Slowly, students offered answers such as "opening credits," "special effects," and "a sound track." Though as Samuel Crowl asserts, "The camera is the single most important technological tool in filmmaking" (xiv), I had to mention the word *camera*, and even then, had to prod their thinking. "How does the use of a camera make film different, very different, from books and plays?" I asked, but from their quizzical faces I could see that these students had much to learn.

Film lexicons are widely available in books and online. Teasley and Wilder provide a compact glossary on page 20 of their book, and John Golden provides a more extensive one in Appendix A of *Reading in the Dark*. In fact, it was Chapter 1 of Golden's book that first gave me a clear and thorough explanation of cinematic terms and the confidence to begin using them in class. Over time, I have borrowed from a number of sources to compile a glossary of film terms (see Handout 3.1) that is comprehensive enough to inform and enrich the limited vocabulary that students bring to the task of describing what they see and hear in film.

To introduce this somewhat intimidating handout to students, I follow Golden's rule that students learn best by doing: I distributed the film glossary along with sheets of scrap paper and told students to read the definitions for camera shots, angles, movement, and editing techniques and to practice them with a rolled-up paper camera lens. Students stood on chairs to practice high-angle shots of their friends and slowly spun themselves to pan the classroom. They placed a student at the front of the room pointing and staring in horror at two other students at the back of the room, one throttling the other to fictional death, and "shot" an eye-line match of the student witnessing the crime, then of the crime itself, then back to the distraught student witness.

One year later, colleague Bill Drewnowski would update the hands-on component of this introductory lesson by having his students practice the elements of cinematography described in Handout 3.1, not with rolled-up scrap paper but with the cameras in their cell phones. After they reviewed the glossary and viewed examples of almost every term by watching the opening scene of the pilot of the television show *Lost* (a clip Drewnowski highly recommends for this lesson), students paired up and each team drew a couple of terms randomly out of a hat. "They were responsible for creating a ten-second film clip demonstrating the terms they had drawn—camera shot, angle, focus, movement, et cetera," Drewnowski explained. So that each team could focus on cinematography, the theatrical element—the actors, costumes, and set—consisted of a collection of toys and action figures housed in his classroom.

After filming their toy stories, students emailed their clips to Drewnowski and they viewed them together on the SMART Board. Though cell phone use is banned at our school, this creative teacher found an academically sound reason to break the rules.

Handout 3.2 is a summary of the questions that guide an exploration of film in the English classroom. After students play with the definitions on the film glossary, it's helpful to return to small groups and to those top ten lists and ask students to read the cinematic question set and discuss the cinematic techniques they now recall from their favorite movies. What about the camera work, editing, lighting, and sound can they recall as being particularly memorable? In my classroom, one group recalled the shot sequence of a car chase, not with the precision of a cinematographer's eye but with an eye newly focused on the ways in which the sequence of camera shots can tell a story without words. Another group talked about the ways in which the volume of the musical sound track increases in relation to the intensity of dramatic action.

But at the end of this introductory lesson, we must come to terms with a difficult truth: reading the text and subtext of great literature is hard, but reading film is harder because it is a medium that deliberately effaces itself. "It is a situation perhaps unique to the art of cinema," explains Patrick J. Cook, author of *Cinematic* Hamlet, "that an increased familiarity with a [film] does not imply greater awareness of its methods" (9). To stay the ghost of film, to learn how the camera and sound equipment "add another 'language' to the text" (Cartmell 6), it is best to begin reading film with still and silent images. Chapters 1 and 2 begin the process with a focus on the principles of photography: framing, placement, subject arrangement, lighting, and color. Here, our swift scene flies to cinematography.

Seeing Shakespeare's Three Faces

Before attempting to read a Shakespeare film clip, I divide students into literary teams, theatrical teams, and cinematic teams, and give each team a set of publicity stills. (Publicity and film stills from both recent and past film productions are widely available on the Internet.) Using Handout 3.2 as the first guide to their critical viewing—and reminding students to temporarily translate the word *film* on the handout into *film images*—students analyze the images in their teams and then share their observations with the whole group.

In our reading of publicity stills published at the PBS *King Lear* website, one literary group was struck by the symbolism in an image from the opening scene in which Lear, enraged by Cordelia's refusal to take part in her father's Who-loves-me-best? contest, disowns her and tells her suitors that Cordelia's dowry will be "Nothing: I have sworn" (1.1.245). They pointed out the symbolism of Lear's crown held to his face like a zero. Calling upon Michael Witmore's brilliant analysis in *Shakespearean Metaphysics* and "the strange power of nothing to measure something" (64) in *King Lear*, I told students that the word *nothing* is repeated more than thirty times in this play. They also noted the symbolism of color, with Lear dressed in power red and Cordelia in purest white.

Two weeks earlier, when we had read to the end of act 2, I had assigned students to design before-and-after costumes for a character in this play who undergoes a dramatic change in status—King Lear, Kent, Edgar, Goneril, or Regan (see Handout 3.3). Students who worked on Lear's costume concluded from the language of the play that as Lear becomes less powerful he begins to empathize with the powerless, but they wanted him to keep his crown and royal robes, now dirty and frayed, and they added a cane to show his physical deterioration. In contrast to their own choices, students in one theatrical team admired the way that costume and makeup are used in the PBS production to dramatize not only Lear's deterioration in status but also his degeneration into second childhood. Instead of a crown, Ian McKellan wears a wreath of flowers, and instead of leaning on a cane as some of my students had imagined, he wields the Fool's staff. "He looks older and younger all at once," one student said.

Students in a cinematic group were drawn to an image of McKellan, his face flooded by a light whose source is outside the frame of the image. Using the film glossary to guide them, they thought this might be a low-angle medium shot with front lighting that creates a halo effect, but they weren't entirely sure. One student in the group noted that in spite of the bright light on Lear's hands and face, there are shadows too. "Maybe that's the point," a student said. "Maybe nothing is clear in this play."

Three decades of research on adolescent literacy has established a necessary relationship between vocabulary instruction and comprehension; the need to define and understand words is compounded when the English curriculum expands to include film images, screenplays, storyboards, and film. Even on days when the lesson plan is strictly word first, students can review and apply the glossary of film terms to film stills. Many teachers begin each class by having students complete a short, independent "do-now" or "daily practice" activity, and for this purpose I routinely scour the Internet for film images that challenge students to see like cinematographers (see Handout 3.4). In time I learned to add the term *Effect* to these activities; whether discussing literature or film, teaching students to recognize techniques without wondering about their purpose and power limits understanding.

Unlike daily practice exercises on the topics of vocabulary and grammar, these exercises not only engage students in brief, focused analysis of the diction and syntax of film, but they also generate lively classroom conversations that cause students to keep using the language of film even when we are not engaged in reading film. Handout 3.5 includes three literal comprehension checks that I use during the earliest stage of film vocabulary acquisition.

Introducing students to the principles of visual composition outlined in Chapter 1 (framing, placement, arrangement, lighting, and color), to the three faces of Shakespeare (literary, theatrical, and cinematic), and to the glossary of film terms (camera work, editing techniques, lighting, and sound) is like handing them a jumbled set of keys. At this point, few of my students are ready to unlock cinematic Shakespeare. So we focus first on the more familiar act of looking *into* film for the literary and theatrical faces of Shakespeare film clips. Learning to look *at* film, to focus on the near-invisible methods of camera work and sound design, will take time and practice.

Focusing on the Familiar

At first I wondered if it would feel redundant to ask students to read a film clip of a scene we had just read word first, for the film's literary elements. From a recent immersion in the research on adolescent literacy, I had restructured my lessons for *King Lear* around the active reading roles of reciprocal teaching and literature circles (for a full discussion, see *Reading Shakespeare with Young Adults* [Dakin], Chapter 9, "Reading in Companies"). To help students see that the roles they assume in reading companies are essential parts of our daily, whole-group work in English class, I projected Figure 3.2, a chart I had constructed from my prereading and act 1, scene 1 lesson plans.

Though the chart indicates that our whole-group readings incorporate all of the active reading roles, the greatest focus in our reading of act 1 had been, and almost always is, on characterization. If adolescent readers can't be inspired to wonder about the characters they meet in act 1 of any play by William Shakespeare, if they cannot begin to see themselves mirrored, then the work of language and conflict analysis will be mechanical for them. Yet in spite of this focus, throughout our reading of the first act students had been oversimplifying the character of Goneril; I couldn't help but think that although no one spoke it aloud, they were defaulting en masse to the "b-word" as an easy, prepackaged label for a character that, at least in act 1, is morally ambiguous.

So I chose a clip from act 1, scene 4 on the DVD in which Goneril divests her father of his knights, because in this production Frances Barber, the actor who plays Goneril, conveys a vulnerability that might

Literature Circle Roles	Act 1.1
Connector	Prereading: Draw your kingdom. Divide it. Who will inherit the divisions? What will you ask for in return?
Illustrator	Prereading: Diagram the cast list as a family tree.
Vocabularian	Prereading: Check for understanding of the multiple meanings of *dowry, breed, banish, bond.*
Character Captain	Act 1.1.1–33: Characterize Gloucester. Act 1.1.134–213: Character- ize Kent. Throughout the act, we will indirectly characterize the sisters, Burgundy, France, and Lear. We will discuss relationships, notably Lear's relationship with Cordelia and his attitude toward her suitors.
Director	Stage direction after line 33: Visualize this entrance as festive, as ceremonial, as tense (Bain 54). Ask questions throughout the reading for staging: Where does Edmond stand as his father jokes about his illegitimacy? Where does Cordelia stand in relation to her sisters? What is Cordelia doing as Lear shames her in front of her suitors?
Questioner	"Love and be silent" (1.1.68): Is there something about love that is essentially inexpressible?
Wordsmith	Monitor the pronoun shifts (the royal *we*, the 2nd person familiar) throughout and discuss tone. After first reading, chunk the scene into three chunks that correlate with the shifts from prose to verse to prose. Note repetitions of: nothing, eyes, sight, seeing, see, speak, speech.
Literary Luminary	Kent's pun on the meanings of *conceive*: 1.1.12 Word families and the language of commerce (*dower, price, wealth,* etc.): 1.1.215–89 France's antithesis, "Thou art most rich, being poor . . .": 1.1.290–303 Allusions to Greek and Roman gods
Prophet	Predict the consequences of Lear's love contest: 1.1.37–59. Predict what may happen in this play at the end of act 1.
Summarizer	Postreading: Summarize the scene as a fairy tale/6 o'clock news/ gossip/cartoon/poem or nursery rhyme/rap lyrics
Reciprocal Teaching Roles	Questioner, Clarifier, Summarizer, Predictor, Connector

Figure 3.2. Reading company roles chart.

influence viewers to read her as sympathetic, or at the very least as more complex. We worked together with the clip, viewing it first to focus on the literary elements of the scene, using Handout 3.2 as a guide, and then a second time to more closely read the theatrical elements.

After the first viewing, students discussed the literary elements— *Who are the characters in this clip? What's the setting? What happens here? What's wrong?*—with relative ease. But when I asked about the characterization of Goneril, students expressed surprise at the actor's crying and the camera's inclination to focus on her face more than on Lear's. Even after a first viewing, they were noticing elements of the theatrical and cinematic. The notes of our whole-class conversation indicate that in this first round of reading the literary elements of the film clip, students' perceptions of Lear's oldest daughter were shifting:

> *Characters*: Lear, Goneril, Albany, Fool, a servant, Oswald
>
> *Setting*: Inside Gloucester's castle
>
> *Plot*: Lear and Goneril fight over the knights. Lear curses Goneril.
>
> *Tones*: Formal, tense, angry, enraged, calculating (in roughly this order)
>
> *POV*: Goneril—the camera focuses on her, and her crying creates more sympathy for her.
>
> *Audience*: The scene appeals to older viewers and educated people who have read the play. It might appeal to fans of Ian McKellan. Emotionally, it appeals to people who have been taken advantage of (some students cite Goneril as the person being taken advantage of, others cite Lear).
>
> *Mood*: Sad, dark
>
> *Symbols*: The ripping paper and white handkerchief
>
> *Theme*: Loyalty, respect and disrespect, revenge

Before our second viewing, I distributed Handout 3.6 and randomly assigned students to focus on one of the five bulleted elements of the theatrical. If students needed to take notes during our viewing, they could, though I encouraged them to postpone note-taking until after we had viewed the same clip a second time. Once students had written down their observations of the actors, costumes, makeup, set, props, lighting, color, and sound, the classroom conversation bubbled into a debate with more incisive comments on details they had only superficially noted in the first viewing.

Some students read a cold and calculating Goneril and some read a character so deeply traumatized by her father's curse of childlessness that the sound of her letter being crumpled in Lear's hands becomes the sound in her mind's ear of her reproductive organs drying up! These extreme readings of Goneril bring to mind Louise Rosenblatt's point that what readers bring to the text—in this case, a verbal and visual text—is at least as powerful as the text itself (78). I collected and collated their notes for a shared reading the next day:

Actors: Goneril's face looks extremely angry—her stare is very intimidating. Her line delivery is sharp—every word cuts. At the end, when she says "I know his heart," you believe her. Lear has trouble speaking. Lear seems lost or drunk, which contributes to his line delivery until Goneril hands him a letter; then he turns extremely angry and yells. Before the curse, Goneril smirks at Lear's breakdown. After the curse, she is clearly shaken and she speak-cries, but not when her father returns to the room. The age of the actor seems to show that her biological clock is ticking and if she doesn't get pregnant soon, she never will. Lear and Goneril each play their characters as split personalities, filled with extreme emotions—they yell, cry, command.

Costumes, makeup: Lear's costume is a red and gold military coat, but it's beginning to look raggedy. Only Lear wears red; the others stick to blacks and greys. Goneril's gown is formal and made of dark material like silk. Her hair is pulled back to reveal her sharp features. Her makeup emphasizes extremes—a very white face and very red lips. Albany's suit is dark but trimmed with gold; there's a tie around Albany's neck like a noose or leash?

Set and props, lighting and color: The set is dark and shadowy. The brightest lit object is Lear's white hair. When light hits Goneril's face, it reveals sadness and disappointment. The props include a flask, bags and books, a handkerchief, and letters—props not in Shakespeare's text. Lear drinks from a flask that he took from the Fool. Goneril hands Lear a letter as part of her command—he waves it in the air, and when he curses her, he crumples it up. She grabs her waist when he does this, as if something inside her is crumpling up too.

Sound, silence: There are sounds of laughter in the background but they stop when Goneril yells. Then there is mostly silence, which makes Goneril's angry voice stand out. There are quiet animal noises in the background. We hear horse noises while Lear is processing his daughter's plan to "disquantity" his knights—maybe the knights are leaving already. We hear them more loudly when a character says, "Saddle my horses." We can hear people scattering about until they are gone and only Lear's voice is heard. There's a bird noise that is almost scary, like the sound of a scavenger. The sound of ripping paper is dramatic and emphasizes the destruction of this family. Goneril speaks roughly to her husband Albany and calls for Oswald. "I know his heart"—what does she mean? Is Lear's heart bad? Good? She sounds worried, knowing he is powerful and capable of a lot if Regan treats him better than she has.

During this second reading of the film clip, one student even recorded details of the camera work by noting the use of rack focus on Lear and Goneril:

> Sometimes the camera focuses on Lear as he speaks and we see Goneril just behind him, in shadows and out of focus. Then the focus shifts and we see Goneril more sharply than Lear. This makes me think they don't really see each other.

One student, seeing a connection between the camera work and two characters in a dysfunctional relationship in *King Lear*, signaled a small but striking shift in the focus of our classroom reading. In *How to Read Literature like a Professor*, Thomas C. Foster uses the term *intertextuality* to name the "dialogue between old texts and new" (34). If the word *text* includes "media texts aligned to the grade or course curriculum" (Common Core State Standards Guiding Principle 3), and if our students can learn not only to hear the intertextual dialogue between seventeenth-century poet-playwright William Shakespeare and modern directors, actors, and film producers but also to take part in it, to enter the conversation, then their reading will be timeless, rich, and deep.

4 Seeing Double

Methinks I see these things with parted eye,
When everything seems double.
A Midsummer Night's Dream 4.1.196–97

Although Thomas C. Foster writes in the context of literature, the possibilities of intertextuality—"dialogue between old texts and new" (34)—are expanded when the texts are both verbal and filmic and the dialogue is not between authors but between author and *auteurs*, a term used in film studies to name a filmmaker who, like an author, possesses a distinctive style and exercises creative control over the production of a film. Laurence Olivier, Orson Welles, Franco Zeffirelli, Kenneth Branagh, Julie Taymor, and Michael Almereyda, to name just a few, have all been influenced by their predecessors in filmmaking, and when they take up the same Shakespeare text—*Hamlet* or *Henry V*, for example—they find ways to pay homage to both the playwright and the filmmakers who inspired them.

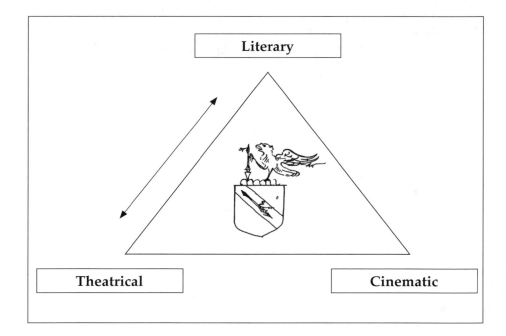

Literary

Theatrical

Cinematic

Even as they seek comparison with past masters, great directors and actors pursue a creative contrast that gives us a rich and strange array of comparative performances. Before focusing on the third and least familiar of Shakespeare's faces, the cinematic, students gain greater confidence in their ability to explore the new possibilities of Shakespeare on film when they focus first on the literary and the theatrical.

In expanding the intertextual dialogue to include two or more performances of the same speech or scene on film, we can compare what we have already read and discussed in class for the theatrical choices that extend the debate on Shakespeare's dynamic literary text. Viewing multiple film clips of a single speech or scene does much more than clarify. In fact, it complicates: students return from film to Shakespeare's text with renewed respect for its myriad possibilities and a greater sense of the active construction that reading Shakespeare requires.

Extreme Reading

Bottom the weaver in *A Midsummer Night's Dream* is a character who inspires extreme readings among scholars, directors, actors, teachers, and students. After we have read act 1, scene 2 and met the Mechanicals, I begin the process of reading this singular character plurally by asking the question "Who's in charge?" followed immediately by "and how can you tell?" The answers are not always obvious, and the question is critical to an understanding of group dynamics in a Shakespeare play. Students have heard the question before, with the entrance of the three witches in *Macbeth*, Rosencrantz and Guildenstern in *Hamlet*, and the Shipmaster, Boatswain, mariners, and nobles in the opening scene of *The Tempest*. For clues to potential answers, we reread the stage directions; note which character gets the first, last, and/or best lines in the scene; note who asks questions and who answers them; note uses of the second-person familiar pronoun *thou-thee-thy-thine* and the implications of power and status these pronouns imply; consider shifts from verse to prose and vice versa; and tally the number of lines a character speaks.

Students quickly detect a tug-of-war between Quince the carpenter and Bottom the weaver but disagree on the tone of their relationship. When I ask them to generate a list of character traits for each, Peter Quince usually earns the nobler attributes—"patient, hard-working, smart"—and Nick Bottom lands the lesser—"cocky, obnoxious, foolish." When I confess that Bottom is one of my favorite characters in all of Shakespeare, I'm usually able to wring from at least one student the half-hearted compliment, "Well, he's sort of funny. He thinks he can play Pyramus *and* Thisbe *and* the Lion." *Enter* Kevin Kline, who when offered the part of Bottom in the 1999 Michael Hoffman film production, "countered with the suggestion that he could play Theseus, Oberon, *and* Bottom" (Buchanan 141). Perfect!

At this early stage in our reading of the play as literary and theatrical text, we view a single film clip of this scene as both an introduction to the genre of Shakespeare comedy (act 1, scene 1 reads more like a tragedy) and as an introduction to reading Shakespeare on film. Guided by Handout 3.6, students watch the Hoffman film clip and notice how the facial expressions, vocal tones, actions, and gestures of the actors construct a reading of the Mechanicals that gently humanizes them all, but especially Nick Bottom, who begins the scene posing like a gentleman in a white suit but by scene's end is stained with red wine spilled on him by a mocking boy. In addition to the operatic sound track and the bustling, sun-drenched set, students read a wordless back story for Bottom composed not by William Shakespeare but by Hoffman's camera, suggesting that Bottom is married to a bitter shrew and loved hopelessly from afar by a gentle and sympathetic young woman.

"What character traits does Kevin Kline emphasize in his portrayal of Bottom in this scene?" I ask. "He's a dreamer," Lindsay says. Perfect, I think to myself.

After we have read act 4, scene 1 for the literary elements of Bottom's dream, and after students debate where Bottom stands in a continuum from static and asinine to dynamic and spiritually awakened, I distribute Handout 4.1 and students collaborate on what for most of them is a new genre of writing, the screenplay. Though some professional screenplays include specific information about camera shots, many screenwriters prefer to leave those decisions to the director and camera operators (Blacker 70); in Handout 4.1 the directions for writing slug lines are limited to the three most basic pieces of information. (For more on writing screenplays in the secondary classroom, see Chapter 11 of *Reading Shakespeare with Young Adults* [Dakin].) After students have assumed the role of screenwriter and developed their own vision of Bottom's dream, we view two very different performances of the same speech by James Cagney in the 1935 Reinhardt-Dieterle production and Kevin Kline in the 1999 production. To better see the compare-and-contrast nature of their notes, I modified Shakespeare's triangle into a chart, Handout 4.2.

When the objective is more specific—when, for example, we want students to compare their word-first reading of the literary element of setting, conflict, theme, or genre to potentially contrary theatrical readings in two or more film clips—it can be useful to narrow the field of vision by constructing more specialized viewing guides.

Focused Viewing

Othello is one of Shakespeare's plays whose opening scene is problematic for adolescent readers: it begins in medias res, and Iago's long opening speech lays out the lines of an intricate military and political plot. Interrupted several times by a gentleman named Roderigo, who is neither military nor political yet somehow has a stake in these matters, Iago's speech is riddled with vague pronoun references. For example, in the sequence of lines 1.1.13–19, "But *he*, as loving *his* own pride and purposes, / Evades *them* . . . and what was *he*?" (emphasis added), Iago refers to at least three different players in the intrigue—Othello, Iago's political mediators, and rival Michael Cassio. The odd confrontation with Brabantio, "*above*" and then at street level; the bestial references to Othello and Desdemona; and Iago's refusal to name Othello anything other than "the Moor" and "his Moorship" immediately contribute to the psychological, cultural, and racial complexity of Iago's resentment and to the theme of appearances and reality that will drive this play to its nightmarish end.

In all the years I have taught this play, I have rarely worked with students who can immediately answer the question, "What do you know about Venice? How can the setting immediately contribute to a viewer's comprehension of what it took us a whole class period to begin to understand—the language, the characters, the conflicts and themes?" Of course, this question asks too much too soon, but it moves students from what they know about the more familiar literary elements of Shakespeare's text into the less familiar territory of theatrical and cinematic Shakespeare. To get students into the act of transmediation, "the translation of meaning across sign systems" (McCormick 580), I ask them to grapple with the limitations—labyrinthine language, complex characters, lots of talking and little action—of this and other opening scenes in Shakespeare by representing the language in concrete and vivid ways:

> Beyond its theatrical limitations, what are the theatrical possibilities of this scene? How could we translate the language of this scene into a set, props, costumes, and sounds that both draw in an audience and help them to understand the characters, conflicts, and themes of this play?

Students use the classroom computer to search for images of Venice and project them onto the SMART Board. The artists in the room sketch a stage set on the side whiteboard that incorporates our best ideas. If time permits, we edit the dialogue down to what will be the opening minutes of the "two hours' traffic of our stage": I project the text and we slash Iago's long speeches by as much as 50 percent, keeping only the most dramatic and essential lines.

Though now is not the time to focus on the power of editing to reshape and manipulate the text, film scholar Deborah Cartmell notes surprising differences in line cuts between the Orson Welles 1952 film production of *Othello* and Oliver Parker's 1995 film. In her comparative analysis of the act 1, scene 3 edited dialogue in each sound track, she notes that Welles's Desdemona keeps only one-third of her lines, whereas Parker's Desdemona retains about four-fifths of hers; on the other hand, Welles tends to edit out lines spoken by the Duke to Othello that have "obvious racist overtones," while Parker does not (Cartmell 84). Our purpose at this time with this scene is to clarify and condense.

When one student suggested that the audience should receive a program when they enter "our" theater with scene summaries to help them understand, we brainstormed for a whole-group summary of 1.1: "Welcome to Venice. Bitter that General Othello, a Moor, has promoted Michael Cassio over him, Lieutenant Iago begins his revenge by telling Senator Brabantio that his young, white daughter Desdemona has run away with 'an old black ram.'" We talk about costumes and props. We cast famous celebrities in the parts of Iago, Roderigo, and Brabantio. From reading to staging, we inch our way toward film.

"The truth is," writes Nikos Theodosakis, filmmaker and author of *The Director in the Classroom*, "I am always pitching" (119). From the sender-message-receiver circuitry of the rhetorical triangle to the interior of a film production office, we are always in some stage of constructing projects, describing them in vivid detail, and convincing others to support our work. Inspired by the process Theodosakis outlines in his book, I project this message in my Shakespeare classroom:

Make the Pitch!
You are a young, unknown director with two minutes to
convince a famous film producer that you should be
the next film director of
Othello.
Your film will be spoken in Shakespeare's language. You will
set it in either the past, the present, or the future.
Sketch a storyboard that you will show to the famous producer
to illustrate your ideas about the opening scene.

> You will have two minutes to pitch your vision of the opening
> scene of *Othello*.
> Good luck!

A variety of storyboard templates is available online and in print. Theodosakis provides a simple preproduction storyboard template in his book and John Golden provides a very helpful two-step storyboard template in *Reading in the Dark*. But long before I had these, I would simply distribute scrap paper to students and have them fold it into six roughly equal blocks; when flattened out, it looks like the blank cells in a page from a comic book or graphic novel. Using stick figures, students sketch a frozen frame of film into each block, accompanied by a line of dialogue written at the bottom of each block to indicate what viewers hear as they see each frame of film. For a fuller discussion of reading Shakespeare onto film, see Chapter 8.

Although students could spend an entire class period working on their storyboards and their pitch, I hurry them so that we can engage in a whole-group discussion of the possibilities of our new-hatched ideas. Though each team pitches its storyboard, at this time, it is not my objective to have students continue the process by engaging in a production project but only to become familiar with the process and to view comparatively their ideas alongside the ideas of Shakespeare filmmakers. For a discussion of how to involve students in a production project, see Chapter 8.

Using Handout 4.3 to guide our viewing, we watch the opening minutes of several *Othello* film productions, though not in chronological order by date of production. I begin with Parker's 1995 film because, though provocative, it feels more familiar to students since it is crafted much like the tense and mysterious beginnings of films that students are accustomed to watching. The film set convinces students that this production was filmed on location in Venice, and their notes include vivid details of a dark place where masked and curtained people glide by in gondolas to mysterious destinations. They note that a rat runs across Desdemona's path as she hurries to find an inner room, perhaps a chapel, and sanctuary from a threatening world. They describe the costumes as historical and richly detailed, and note that the tense music of the sound track is punctuated by environmental sounds of dripping and splashing water. One student wrote that Kenneth Branagh's voice "simmers with emotion, and when he shouts obscenities at Brabantio, he sounds like he enjoys being crude."

From there we usually move to Trevor Nunn's 1990 filmed stage production, in which the theatrical set makes little attempt to suggest

Venice. Students note the more modern costumes and list Iago's cigarette as an effective prop because, in the words of one student, "the smoke is like a smokescreen that Iago can hide behind." After students hear the heavily edited script in the Parker production, the sound that most immediately strikes them here is the sheer quantity of words in this barely edited script.

Orson Welles's acclaimed 1952 black-and-white film produces a compelling third clip because the film is so different from the first two. Students are visibly perplexed—*Is this what we just read?*—and their notes are often punctuated with question marks: "Looks like a military fortress right on the ocean. What happened to the canals?" The set is all bright sky and dark forms: buildings and people, a procession, a cross, chains, and a cage. Actors wear cloaks and hoods; a body appears, upside down, and then another. The music, composed by Alberto Barberis and Angelo Lavagnino, is heavy and haunting. One student questioned, "The sound is distorted—is it vocals or music? Are the sounds even human?" Students don't understand that they are watching in Welles's opening scene a flash-forward to an unwritten phantasmagoric epilogue of the play.

Tim Blake Nelson's 2001 film *O* provides students with an opportunity to see and hear the opening scene of *Othello* transmediated not only into film but also into popular culture. Though there seems to be no agreement among scholars on what to call them, there are films that make reference to Shakespeare's plays, or in the words of film scholar Deborah Cartmell, "films which just sneak into the Shakespeare-on-film canon" (111). Shakespeare spin-offs are films spoken in modern English and set in the present (of the film's production era) that "shadow the plot" (Buchanan 109) of the play and sometimes, though rarely, shadow Shakespeare's language too. Welles's flash-forward to an act 5 epilogue never written by Shakespeare is compounded in Nelson's film by four centuries and two continents, and students are drawn into this story of *Othello* obliquely yet powerfully as they try to untangle the imagery of doves and hawks, a haunting aria, the warfare of prep school athletes, and the dialogue between old texts and new.

What's Funny?

Though we call it the First Folio, the title of the complete works published in London in 1623 is *Mr. William Shakespeares Comedies, Histories, & Tragedies*, and if nothing else, these three labels in this order approximate the chronology of Shakespeare's development as a writer. In the first decade of his career, he tended to produce more comedies and histories, in the second decade, more tragedies (McDonald 80). But it doesn't take a title to know that in Shakespeare, the modes are mixed. What's funny in Shakespeare? The answer is complicated.

Read this paragraph in the form of an *Aside* because its author is ill-prepared to explain what she herself barely understands—bioinformatics, multivariate statistics, and text-tagging software. Nonetheless, Tom Post of *Forbes Magazine* reports on groundbreaking research led by Michael Witmore, director of the Folger Shakespeare Library in Washington, DC, and former head of the Working Group for Digital Inquiry at the University of Wisconsin–Madison. "If you ask a highly linguistically informed computer program to give you a description of what makes comedy comedy," Witmore explains, you will learn, among many other things, that Shakespeare consistently employs the linguistic conventions of comedy in the tragedies. Furthermore, if you plot his thirty-seven plays into clusters, as Witmore and Matthew L. Jockers, codirector of the Stanford Literary Lab, did, you will find the comedy *A Midsummer Night's Dream* in the tragedy cluster (Jockers).

Perhaps Shakespeare's linguistic juxtapositions are the unconscious reason why we laugh so uncomfortably so often at a Shakespeare comedy. At this writing, I haven't found a way to incorporate the new research on digitized Shakespeare into our exploration of genre, but we need to wonder at the possibilities.

Before looking for the comic potential in a Shakespeare scene, start with the familiar. Write the names of students' favorite comic actors on the board and brainstorm for the things these actors do that make them funny. Then preface the focused viewing of a comic Shakespeare scene by projecting this question:

> Beyond the text itself, and the jokes in Shakespeare's text can be difficult to get, what theatrical elements can contribute to a comic performance of this scene?

As I have done with *A Midsummer Night's Dream,* locate two or more film productions of a great comic scene in the play you are reading and distribute Handout 4.4, modified to the play and scene you have chosen. Along with the Reinhardt-Dieterle 1935 film production and the 1999 Hoffman production, I sometimes add a third viewing of the 1982 Joseph Papp New York Shakespeare Festival production, directed by James Lapine. Students thoroughly enjoy the theatrical elements of this Central Park performance.

In their focused notes on the 1935 production, my students consistently commented on the contrasts between the working-class

Mechanicals and the nobility, and though they described the slapstick performance of the play-within-the-play with words such as *awkward, giggling, exaggerated,* and *silly,* it is the line delivery and costumes of the noble audience that make this my students' least favorite production. Students who focused on acting and costumes objected to the way in which the Mechanicals, in their roles as Pyramus, Thisbe, Wall, Moonshine, and Lion, are made to look "stupid and ridiculous" in comparison to their social betters. In reading through their commentary, I was reminded of the rhetorical triangle and the fact that any change in the speaker-message-audience dynamic sends a ripple effect through the other two. In this case, the directors' glamour-craved, Depression-era audience was now a roomful of twenty-first-century high school students, and they resented what they perceived as the validation of a privileged and arrogant upper class. "Hippolyta's headgear is strange, her huge collar is ridiculous, and the King wears fur and a crown, like the burger King," Yasmen wrote.

In contrast, student notes on the theatrical elements of Hoffman's 1999 film production were consistently positive: "Comical mistakes, awkward sexual allusions that I didn't get when I read them, funny costumes, a spinning-flying dog . . ." These are just some of the theatrical elements of this performance that Lindsay listed in her notes. When Flute, made up to play Thisbe with "big red cheeks, red lips, eye-shadow, and a beard," and consistently mocked by his sophisticated audience, finds his dead Pyramus, drops his fake voice at the line, "O Pyramus, arise," and takes off his wig, these young viewers were visibly surprised and satisfied too. "At that moment, all three of the worlds that are represented in this play," Marissa noted, "are equal, in a comical and sad way."

Each time I ask students a question I used to think was simple— "What's funny?"—the answers make me remember the Hollywood legend of an old actor's last words, "Dying is easy. Comedy is hard."

Virtual Seeing

In a delightful twist on the act of seeing double, English teacher and author Lynette Williamson outlines in an article for *English Journal* how she challenges her students to assume the perspective of a patron at the Globe Theatre by choosing a virtual seat in one of the three stratified sections of Shakespeare's professional home. Although a scarcity of demographic information has fueled disagreement about the typical Elizabethan audience, scholar Russ MacDonald affirms that "most social classes, from apprentices to gallants, were . . . among the 3,000 people who packed the Globe for Shakespeare's most popular plays" (118–19). Playing with the distinct possibility that, at the same performance, an illiterate servant or a prostitute could be standing in the "yard" or pit as a merchant and his wife sit in the lower gallery and a lord and lady recline in the uppermost private galleries above the stage, Williamson's students adopt the social class of an audience member before they view a film adaptation of a Shakespeare play they are reading. After viewing, they keep a journal written from the perspective of the Elizabethan audience member whose seat they have chosen to occupy.

Take a Virtual Seat . . .

in the pit
if you are a "groundling" who attends productions for their special effects. You should note scenes of violence, gore, sex, and dirty jokes.

in the gallery
if you are an educated member of the middle class who appreciates the intricacies of the plot. You should note puns, riddles, ironies, juxtapositions, and double entrendres.

in the balcony seats above the stage
if you are a noble or member of the royalty. You should note scenes of political intrigue, the foibles of the rich and powerful, and the royals' place in the Great Chain of Being. (73)

Even as students play and write their parts with creative abandon, they experience viscerally the energy field symbolized by the rhetorical triangle and the myriad ways in which authors and directors appeal to multiple audiences. "When students take a virtual seat," Williamson affirms, "they are practicing multiple layers of aesthetic appreciation: an appreciation for Shakespeare, an appreciation for film, and an appreciation for the artistic choices directors make" (72).

No author is more acutely aware of the instability of words, the complexity of verbal and nonverbal codes, and the necessity of collaboration than William Shakespeare. Reading the plays word first requires continuous refocusing because his text is inherently unstable. From without, there are multiple versions of eighteen of the plays in the form of quartos published during his lifetime; even the stability of the Folio, published by colleagues seven years after his death, has been called into question. Since the nineteenth century, the authorship of the plays has been periodically challenged, and candidates for the honor have included Christopher Marlowe; Sir Francis Bacon; Edward de Vere, Earl of Oxford;

and Queen Elizabeth I (McDonald 197, 24). In the 2011 "political thriller" *Anonymous*, director Roland Emmerich makes the case for de Vere.

From within, the collection of thirty-seven plays lacks a narrator, and their early modern English author speaks in tongues: according to data collected at the Open Source Shakespeare website, the plays contain the speaking parts for 1,221 characters. Deciphering where Shakespeare stands on themes of life and death, of gender, race, religion, power, and politics, is almost anyone's guess, though tantalizing patterns do emerge. His characters "embrace contrary natures" (Costanzo 168) and invite extreme readings; consider, for example, "Hamlet, the (melancholic, witty, heroic, hypocritical, rational, vengeful, compassionate, cruel, amiable, determined, undecided, mad, wise) Prince of Denmark" (Mellor 57). The playwright composed minimal directorial commentary in the form of fragmentary stage directions such as *Enter, Exit*, and *Retires.*

As students learn to read and view Shakespeare's text for its continuously new possibilities, and as they become more practiced viewers of the literary and theatrical faces of Shakespeare on film, they will slowly but surely acquire a third eye that empowers them not only to look into but also to look *at* Shakespeare on film (Cook 9).

5 Reading, Refocused

Mine eyes are made the fools o' th' other senses,
Or else worth all the rest.

Macbeth Act 2.1.56–57

I t was the preposition *at* in the title *Looking at Movies: An Introduction to Film* (Barsam and Monahan), that made me doubt, though briefly, the perspective of a 600-page textbook on the elements of filmmaking. *At* implies the celluloid surface of film, a surface I thought I could see. Then I saw, slowly, the authors' point: we are far more likely to fall headlong *into* film, confounded by the invisibility of its methods, transfixed by its constantly shifting visual field, and biased by a visceral identification with the human faces of characters whose points of view we vicariously adopt through the camera lens, than to labor analytically at the surface.

With literature and theater, we are conscious of ourselves as both involved in and apart from the story, but the resources of cinema—close-up shots, camera angles, a layered sound track, seamless editing

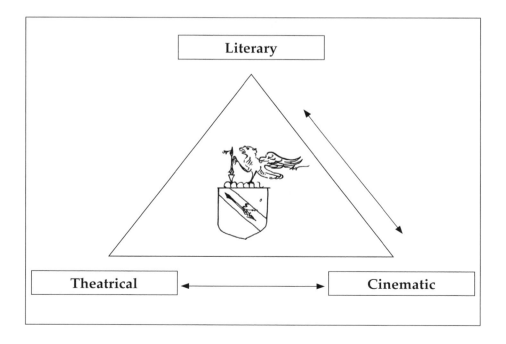

techniques—appeal directly to subliminal responses and powerful instinctive drives. "Often imperceptible," explain Richard Barsam and Dave Monahan, "cinematic language, composed not of words but of myriad integrated techniques and concepts, connects us to the story while deliberately concealing the means by which it does so" (3). How and why we learn to look *at* the cinematic face of Shakespeare is the subject of this chapter.

While adapting Shakespeare's *Hamlet* to screenplay, director Michael Almereyda came to see it as his "main job . . . to imagine a parallel visual language that might hold a candle to Shakespeare's poetry" (Almereyda x). Though my first love will always be words, words, words, I have come to appreciate how the transmediation of Shakespeare's words into film images and sound continually renews both his art and ours.

Focusing on the Unexpected

Beyond learning the functional, high-frequency vocabulary of film and recognizing the methods of filmmaking by looking at film stills, we need to practice seeing the methods in their natural and most powerful context, the moving sequence of variable frames. In contrast to the relatively fixed frame of a stage or a book, film assembles the building blocks of narrative (chapters, scenes, acts) into thousands of shots that employ a near-infinite variety of camera shots, angles, movement, focus, and editing techniques, all of which are intensified by an equally rich and subtle sound design.

As Patrick J. Cook, film scholar and professor of English at George Washington University, points out in *Cinematic* Hamlet, the modern, unabridged text of *Hamlet* is composed of "nineteen discrete scenes punctuated by the emptying of the stage," whereas Olivier's film "assembles 433 shots . . . that interpret, focus interest, and facilitate the construction" of meaning (17–18). Olivier's *Hamlet* was released in 1948; since the middle of the twentieth century, the trend in filmmaking has been to create longer films with more shots of shorter length. The final edited version of a typical modern movie will be composed of two thousand to three thousand shots, and the ratio of unused to used shots can often be twenty to one, meaning that for every single minute of film we see, twenty minutes of footage has been deleted (Barsam and Monahan 322).

Cinematic language almost always seeks to erase its tracks; we wander into a film Hansel-and-Gretel-like, leaving our trail of bread, only to find that the camera has eaten the crumbs and we are lost in the filmic woods. One of the main reasons why film is hard to read is that most of the time, variable framing in a film is "relatively neutral, inexpressive, or conventional" (Cook 15), edited into a sequence of seamless cuts to stationary, eye-level, medium shots in neutral lighting. Cook's basis of analysis is to determine how a director creatively and effectively "maximizes the advantages of the medium" (15). First base in the secondary English classroom is a bit less ambitious: I ask students to notice the unexpected. There will almost always be a correlation between the intensity of our responses to a film and its deviations from the cinematic norm.

Barsam and Monahan define a *shot* as "one *uninterrupted* run of the camera" and a *shot sequence* as "a series of edited shots characterized by inherent unity of theme and purpose" (557). Often, the literary and theatrical concept of a single scene in Shakespeare will be translated into a series of shot sequences in the film, and the shot sequences may be arranged out of sequence from the play. For example, Almereyda decided that the best way to begin *Hamlet* was not with act 1, scene 1, a platform before Elsinore Castle and a ghost-struck Bernardo speaking, "Who's there?," but with a voice-over of Ethan Hawke in the role of Hamlet, speaking an edited version of Hamlet's prose speech from act 2, "I have of late, but wherefore I know not, lost all my mirth . . ." (2.2.318–34). This structural decision in itself is a deviation from the norm of the literary and theatrical script, and if students have read *Hamlet* they will be prepared to wonder why, but I try to save the whys for later.

I begin to teach students to read shot sequences with the opening sequence of Almereyda's 2000 *Hamlet*. We view it once simply to count the number of shots. Including the first two logo shots[3] ("Miramax Films" / "double A films") and the title shot, "Hamlet," we number as we view, thinking that in the first two and a half minutes of film, there are twenty-two shots in the opening shot sequence, though there is some confusion about the four different titles overlaid onto the first establishing shot.

Before the second viewing, I distribute Handout 5.1 and explain that when directors do the unexpected, their purpose is to intensify our response to key elements of their film. *Our* purpose is to learn to see the unexpected in a film clip and to connect what we see to what we think and feel about the setting, a character, a speech, an event, or a theme in the film adaptation of Shakespeare's text. It is also helpful, in advance of the second viewing, to have students highlight the cinematic norms of variable framing (formatted here in **bold**) on their film glossary (Handout 3.1) as they prepare to focus on deviations from the norm:

FRAMING/CAMERA SHOTS: **Medium shot**

CAMERA ANGLES: **Eye level**

CAMERA MOVEMENT: **Pan**, **Tilt**, and **Zoom** because each is accomplished using "a camera mounted on the gyroscopic head of a **stationary** tripod" (Barsam and Monahan 249, emphasis added)

EDITING TECHNIQUES: **Cut**

LIGHTING: **Neutral**

Now we are ready to view the opening shot sequence a second time and to focus on the unexpected. I encourage students to watch the shot sequence before taking notes and sometimes assign viewing specialists who focus on only one of the five bullets in Handout 5.1.

Beyond the initial confusion about the series of explanatory titles projected onto the first establishing shot—"New York City, 2000"; "The King and C.E.O. of Denmark Corporation is dead"; "The King's widow has hastily remarried his younger brother"; "The King's son, Hamlet, returns from school, suspecting foul play"—students agree that this shot sequence begins with the expected, a highly informative establishing shot that locates the action in the present day and establishes a dark mood. Using the glossary, students think this is a long shot of the New York City skyline taken from the floor of a moving car through the skylight in the car roof, but they struggle to name the camera angle. "What's the opposite of an overhead angle?" Aaron asks.

Students agree that the long and medium shots of Times Square at night show the action in a city that never sleeps, and the close-ups of Hamlet's face show his emotional reactions to the information in the establishing shot, but they express confusion about shots that don't seem related to the cause-effect pattern of the King's death, the widow's remarriage, and the suspicion of foul play. In short, though most students can figure out that the grainy black-and-white shots of Hamlet speaking his prose speech are meant to be a kind of homemade film-within-the-film, they are perplexed by Hamlet's editing: "What's going on with the dinosaur skeleton? The cartoon? The Stealth bomber?" The tempo of the shots seems normal, though "Hamlet takes a long time to start speaking," Jonathan says.

"Did that make you wonder what he was going to say?" I ask.

"Yeh. 'To be or not to be,' but he didn't," Jon replies.

"How about the final shot, the one before the title?" I ask the class. "Does it feel like a closing shot? Does it dissolve and fade to black?"

"No. It cuts to red," Xuyen says, and instantly I think of all the needless death in this play.

We watch the opening shot sequence a third time to listen in on the compelling juxtaposition of sounds and to review the unexpected: the odd camera angle in the establishing shot and its sequence of titles that nearly summarizes act 1; the cuts in Hamlet's home movie to shots of a dinosaur skeleton, a cartoon monster, and the military surveillance-like images of a bomber, its target, and an explosion; the unusually long time it takes Hamlet to begin speaking the prose speech in his video; the visual disconnect between the Hamlet who filmed himself (students think he looks younger in the black-and-white movie clips) and the Hamlet who now edits the footage; and the sudden cut instead of a fade to the vivid red field of the title frame.

How does the unexpected intensify our response to this production and this shot sequence? Some students who read the play in grade 10 remember that something is rotten in Denmark and that a Ghost demands revenge and Hamlet hesitates, and now they connect these things to the strange images of monsters and bomb targets. They are attracted to this Hamlet because he is almost as young and wired as they are. Students are visibly struck by the vivid translation of Shakespeare's world to their commercialized, mediatized own. "Even someone who never read the play," a student remarks, "would be able to read this *Hamlet*." I catch the choice of verbs, and at least for this shot sequence, I have a surprise that contributes to both the how and why of Almereyda's deviations from the norm.

I project the text of the Folger edition of *Hamlet* act 1, scene 1, beginning with the play's eternal question, "Who's there?" We read aloud to Horatio's question at line 26, "What, has this thing appeared again tonight?" and skim to the answer, "*Enter Ghost*," just before line 47. Then I project the edited text of the first two pages of Almereyda's screenplay:

EXT. NEW YORK CITY: TIMES SQUARE – NIGHT
A near-hallucinatory spectacle: traffic, neon, noise.

Amidst surrounding electronic displays, the animated logo for the DENMARK CORPORATION flashes and whirls.

EXT. HOTEL – NIGHT

A sleek modern façade, doorman, revolving doors.

Lights swim across the hotel's identifying metal plaque:

HOTEL ELSINORE
*[INT. HOTEL ELSINORE; LOBBY/SURVEILLANCE DESK – NIGHT
VIDEO MONITOR: THE LOBBY

A cavernous space, in low light. There's a surge of static. The image seems to shiver.

We hear Bernardo's voice muttering off-screen.

> BERNARDO
> Who's there?

No answer.

Two figures appear, walking hand in hand, their joined shadows reflected on the marble floor.

ANGLE ON THE SECURITY DESK

Bernardo, the night watchman, sits stationed before a bank of surveillance monitors, eating take-out Thai food. He looks exhausted. Marcella approaches.

> MARCELLA
> Olla, Bernardo!

> BERNARDO
> (*startled*)
> What, is Horatio there?

Horatio rounds the corner, lighting a cigarette.

> HORATIO
> A piece of him.

> BERNARDO
> Welcome, Horatio. Welcome, good Marcella—

> MARCELLA
> Has this thing appeared again tonight?

> BERNARDO
> I have seen nothing.

> MARCELLA
> Horatio says 'tis but our fantasy
> And will not let belief take hold of him.
> Therefore I have entreated him along
> With us to watch the minutes of the night,
> That, if again this apparition come,
> He may approve our eyes and speak to it.

> HORATIO
> Tush, tush, 'twill not appear.

Bernardo gestures with his chopsticks.

> BERNARDO
> Sit down awhile—

MARCELLA
(*noting the monitor*)
Break thee off. Look where it comes again!

ON THE MONITOR: HOTEL LOBBY

The picture wavers, a ghostly flicker, as Hamlet's Father strides into view, a tall figure, his back to us.

The figure exits one monitor—then enters another, fluttering in the video haze. . . .

"Is this the opening shot sequence that we just watched three times?" I ask. After reviewing page 1 of the screenplay, students agree that at first it is, but someone notices the asterisk that marks an opening bracket in the screenplay, and we see print evidence of the first of many dramatic sequences that were written, filmed, and edited into an early draft of the film, then cut. "Every movie is made three times," Almereyda points out, "in the writing, in the shooting, and in the editing" (xii). Before sharing with students this director's difficult decision to deviate from his own screenplay and begin Shakespeare's most famous play as no one before him had, I let students grapple with the possibilities of why.

One student's earlier comment that almost anyone could immediately "read" this *Hamlet* brings us close to Almereyda's reasons—a Miramax test screening revealed that Shakespeare's language in the original opening shot sequence confused and distanced viewers, so Almereyda decided to sum up in the establishing shot the setting and conflict and to cut almost immediately to close-up shots of a remarkably young, appealing Hamlet speaking a "stripped down" (135) version of an intimate speech, not to Rosencrantz and Guildenstern but directly, through his PixelVision diary, to us. The immediacy of images in this shot sequence and the layered sounds of urban tech, British trip-hop band Morcheeba, and orchestral music "suit the action to the word, the word to the action" (*Hamlet* 3.2.18–19), and in the doing, transfer and translate meaning between worlds.

Hearing the Cinematic

"We'll hear a play tomorrow," Hamlet informs the First Player (2.2.561), redirecting our sight-centered world back to sound. In the same way, colleague and director of humanities Jonathan Mitchell redirects the focus of this lesson from video to audio by having students view the Almereyda opening shot sequence several times but with the audio muted. After several soundless viewings in which students note and discuss the literary elements of the shot sequence—location, characters, conflict, and mood—students pair up and read the text of five speeches from the play, chunked and annotated to advance their literal comprehension (see Handout 5.2), including the one Almereyda chose ("I have of late, but wherefore I know not . . ."), each as a potential voice-over script for the shot sequence:

> 1.2.141–64: "That it should come to this: . . . But break, my heart, for I must hold my tongue."
>
> 1.4.43–62: "Angels and ministers of grace, defend us! . . . Say, why is this? Wherefore? What should we do?"
>
> 2.2.318–34: "I have of late, but wherefore I know not, lost all my mirth, . . . though by your smiling you seem to say so."
>
> 2.2.611–34: "This is most brave, . . . The play's the thing Wherein I'll catch the conscience of the King."
>
> 3.1.64–96: "To be, or not to be— . . . And lose the name of action."

After students agree on the speech best suited to the shot sequence, they read the lyrics and listen to about one minute of four different songs, only one of which is the Morcheeba music that Almereyda layered into the sound track. For this shot sequence, Mitchell selected

> "Mad World" as performed by Gary Jules, written by Roland Orzabal
>
> "Extreme Ways" by Moby
>
> "Let Me See" by Morcheeba
>
> "Wandering Star" by Portishead

Using Handout 5.3, a focused listening guide adapted by Mitchell from a sound rubric written by music teacher Alec Waugh, students debate the suitability of each musical clip with Almereyda's shot sequence and the speech they have chosen from *Hamlet*, and then nominate their choices. Finally, they watch and hear for the first time both the video and audio tracks. *And the best sound track goes to . . . ?* Don't expect agreement!

Mirror, Mirror

It gets personal pretty quickly in film.

Long shots in films continually immerse us in a new and potentially threatening world where we watch, through the camera's eye and even to the edges of wide-screen frames, for any changes in the field of vision that might require our attention and emotional involvement in the action. Film is hard to read in part because it so relentlessly triggers what cognitive psychologists call the "orienting response," a subliminal survival mechanism for threat assessment that kept our human ancestors alive (Cook 12–13, 15).

Close-up shots in films relax the orienting response and redirect our attention to the book of the human face, with its capacity for wordless expression; among primates, we excel in our ability to process facial information. Film is hard to read in part because we so readily read the nonverbal cues expressed with the larger-than-life eyebrows, eyes, and mouth of the faces onscreen that we enter the scene viscerally—we *feel* the words and the action. The action in most films, as in video games and professional sports, is normally unacceptable, and so the urge to imitate the action we see is inhibited. But a camera carefully focused on the human form triggers powerful brain cells dubbed "mirror neurons" that connect us wordlessly to others (Cook 14–16). When we watch a person suffer, we adopt that person's point of view and suffer with him or her, and if the person cries, we often cry too. In "Mirror Neurons," reported for *Nova* in 2005, Robert Krulwich observes, "There's a place in my brain . . . whose job it is to live in other people's minds, live in other people's bodies . . . and great actors are the experts in the mirror system."

How does cognitive psychology inform the study of Shakespeare on film in the English classroom? I can offer only limited answers. Beyond learning to see the unexpected in film, I ask students to be aware of some of the cinematic ways in which film holds Hamlet's mirror up to nature and causes us to see ourselves in the action, to vicariously play our part. The orienting response is triggered with long shots, especially shots filmed in 70 mm high-resolution and projected onto a wide screen: our field of vision becomes horizontal instead of vertical and our attention to location, to objects, and to entrances and exits is heightened. Mirror neurons are activated by zoom-ins and close-up shots. But one of the most fascinating ways in which we are drawn subliminally into a film can be found in the sequence and separation of shots a director uses to film a conversation.

Depending on the intensity of the scene, directors can frame a conversation using a sequence of three shots when filming two characters or two groups of participants, illustrated here by Jennifer Sao, who imagined a dramatic conversation sequence between Hamlet and Ophelia:

Objective full shots: The camera shows two characters (also called a two-shot) or more (a three-shot, etc.) together in a single shot, usually a medium or long shot. A film conversation often begins with a full shot to establish an introduction to the conversation. The objective full shot is the most theatrical way, yet in film the most objective and least emotional way, to shoot a conversation.

Semisubjective over-the-shoulder shots: The camera, shot from over the shoulder of Character B, focuses on Character A, usually in medium or close-up range; some part of Character B's body—the shoulder, neck, head, or hand, for example—can be seen in the shot. Then the camera reverses its point of view, focusing on Character B from over the shoulder of Character A. This is

the most common way to film a conversation between two characters, and it usually conveys greater emotion because of the opportunity for close-ups and the tendency of viewers to adopt the camera's point of view and to see what a character sees.

Subjective separation shots: The camera separates the characters as they converse, shooting one, then the other in a sequence of three or more eye-line matches; usually each shot is a close-up. This is usually the most intense way to shoot a conversation on film because of the repetition of close-ups

and because the viewer literally stands in, playing the part of the character "behind" the camera. In short, we participate in the conversation, projecting our own reactions and interpretations, our hopes and fears, upon the camera character.

Objective full shot: The camera once again shows the participants together in a single shot, usually medium or long, to establish a resolution to the conversation (Sharff 59–65; Cook 16–17; Dick 52–54).

When we watch two Shakespeare characters engaged in an intense film conversation—for example, Lady Macbeth's desperate dialogue with Macbeth in act 2, scene 2 in the minutes after he has killed his king, or Hamlet's dumbstruck reaction to the Ghost's tale of murder most foul in act 1, scene 5—students can view the film clip once, monitoring the intensity of their emotional response to the characters. Then display and discuss images of the three types of conversational shots and shot sequences, and ask students to focus their second viewing on the director's choices.

Even though some students may not feel the level of emotional engagement they were encouraged to feel by the filming process, looking at camera shots for their incremental capacity to make us look at others and see ourselves profoundly connected to the virtual experience deepens our understanding of the subliminal power of cinematic language.

Reading the Cinematic

The first reason why film is hard to read is that it seeks to efface its methods in an onslaught of conventional sequences of photography, lighting, and editing. In our early viewings, the recognition of any film production technique outside of the norm (the norm being a sequence of seamless cuts to stationary, eye-level, medium camera shots in neutral lighting) will mark the beginnings of second sight. A second reason why film is hard to read is that it triggers powerful subliminal responses in the viewer's brain. A third reason why film is both hard and fascinating to read is that it continuously substitutes the language of the original text with visual and cinematic codes and nonverbal sounds:

> **Visual codes**: for example, realistic locations and sets, lighting, color, and dense visual details (called "worldmaking" by David Bordwell [qtd. in Cook 19]) of clothing, jewelry, décor, machinery, and architecture that overload the senses; cultural, historical, and religious objects that symbolize and contemporize ideas and themes

Cinematic codes: for example, left to right movement as the "right" way; camera fade-ins and fade-outs that signify changes in time and space; camera shots and angles that provoke emotion and extend or limit understanding

Nonverbal sounds: for example, environmental sounds and music that intensify and influence or change our understanding of the images and words; silence that actually causes us to listen harder

To look at how these codes not only translate and transfer meaning but also "compete with and replace the words of the source texts" (Cartmell 6), we need to enter the conversation between language and film; we need to become metalinguists.

In Baz Luhrmann's 1996 *Romeo + Juliet*, Verona, Italy, becomes Verona Beach, California; Chorus becomes a television news anchorwoman; and swords become guns engraved with "Sword 9mm series S" on the barrel, but these metaphors are essentially literary and theatrical, the word- and world play of scriptwriters and costume and set designers. We also need to develop an eye and ear for cinematic metaphors, the brain play of directors, camera operators, and sound designers, especially when Shakespeare's language becomes peripheral to the film (Buchanan 234). The Folger edition of *Romeo and Juliet* act 5, scene 3, the cataclysmic scene inside the tomb, contains 321 lines of dialogue, but Luhrmann's sound track retains only 33 lines (Cartmell 54), which is about 10 percent of the text. "If we lose the words," questions Cartmell, "do we lose 'Shakespeare'?" (2). The answer, I think, can be seen in this brief analysis of filmic poetry, with the literary terms from our handouts underlined and the film terms in bold:

Romeo + Juliet. 1996. Directed by Baz Luhrmann. Director of Photography, Donald M. McAlpine. DVD Chapter 1, "The Prologue"; Chapter 27, "Together at Last"

With the word architecture of a sonnet, Shakespeare's Chorus establishes the <u>setting</u> of *Romeo and Juliet* as a place of "new mutiny, Where civil blood makes civil hands unclean." The manic camera work, dense visual details, and sound design in the first two minutes of Luhrmann's film—**crosscutting, flash cutting, panning**, and **zooming** from **close-ups** to **aerial shots** of the <u>characters</u> (their faces and names briefly frozen into titles) and <u>symbols</u> of civil and uncivil power, employing **handheld camera** news flashes of police cars and helicopters, of violent crime and innocent victims, of competing skyscrapers, corporate logos, and a colossal statue of Jesus, narrated first by the professional voice of an on-camera female news anchor and a second time by a less-reassuring male **off-camera voice-over**—reconstruct the Prologue as a postmodern elegy for the new mutinies of our times.

Flash-forward to Chapter 27 of the DVD, to the scene in the tomb, and the camera recomposes the <u>theme</u> of blind love with a heartbreaking sequence of **close-up** and **extreme close-up shots** in which the camera tells us that Juliet is not dead—in extreme close-ups, her eyelids and fingers twitch—but Romeo fails to see what we see because in **parallel editing**, the camera frames his tear-stained face kissing her hand, her neck, her cheek, her lips. In **extreme close-up,** Juliet's eyes open wide; in **close-up**, Romeo drinks from the vial. In **separation shots**, she sees, he sees, too late.

Even if most American teens know Shakespeare "as a screenwriter first and as a dramatist second" (Cartmell 2), I could not have analyzed the cinematic language of Shakespeare on film three years ago, nor could I have asked my students to do so, because for years film remained a familiar stranger in my classroom, a spare and superficial extra. "We are all learners," writes Sara Kajder, author of *Adolescents and Digital Literacies*, "in a literary landscape that is unfamiliar but packed with new possibilities" (14), and each time we take up the text of Shakespeare on film and acquire alongside our students the third eye that reading film requires, we gain a greater understanding of what it means to be literate in the twenty-first century. Even when the screenplay is full-text Shakespeare (for example, director Kenneth Branagh faced the incredible challenge of including all the language of *Hamlet* on a wide, high-resolution 70 mm screen), modern directors compose the frames of their film with camera strokes that parallel and at times intersect the line of words composed by Shakespeare's pen, intensifying and redirecting our response.

To refocus our reading on the methods by which the camera and sound track compose and ultimately recompose Shakespeare I begin with a great scene that has been filmed by many great directors, *Hamlet* 1.4–5, in which the Ghost and Hamlet come face to face for the first time. Especially if students have not read the text, Branagh's adaptation is the best one to start with because though no words are edited, the camera work in this production, along with the cast and sound design, vividly explicate Shakespeare's language, whereas Almereyda's cultural update seeks to "imagine a parallel visual language" (x). Furthermore, asking students to view a Shakespeare film clip without having first read the text helps to focus our attention on the story about a ghost, a father, and a son that is composed not with the pen but with cameras, editing, and sound.

To put the glossary of film terms to work in its most natural context, I constructed Handout 5.4 not so much as a viewing guide to the ways in which a film recomposes Shakespeare's language (analyzing the rhetoric of recomposition is the focus of the next chapter) but as a guide to how, at the level of the tools at its disposal, film composes a story borrowed from Shakespeare. Before viewing the film clips, students organize themselves into viewing teams and each team prepares to focus on one of the bulleted questions in Handout 5.4. After students in each viewing team discuss and share their notes on the cinematic technique they focused on, each team shares with the whole group its best observations of camera shots, camera angles, camera movements and editing, shot sequence, location and objects, lighting and color, or sound design.

What follows are summary analyses of the cinematic language of a great story borrowed from Shakespeare, composed from the collection of notes written by students on Handout 5.4 as well as the notes I have taken of our whole-group discussions:

> *Hamlet*. 1996. Directed by Kenneth Branagh. Kenneth Branagh as Hamlet, Brian Blessed as Ghost. Director of Photography, Alex Thomson. DVD Chapters 11–13.

- The **special effects** in the opening speech, "Angels and ministers of grace, defend us . . . ," are filmed as a chase scene, the camera **panning** Hamlet, who moves from **left of screen to right**, with about forty shots **flash-cut** into the opening **montage.**

- The **sound effects** and **music** underscore the terror of the immediate scene and the sweet sadness of a lost past; the **vocal** effect of the Ghost's voice is unnatural.

- Hamlet is consistently shot from a **high angle** and the Ghost from a **low angle.**

- A visual disconnect between Hamlet and the Ghost is established at the level of the **shots**: there are only two shots in the entire seven-plus minutes in which Hamlet and the Ghost he perceives to be his father are framed together in an **over-the-shoulder shot**, and the first one is brief and violent—the Ghost's hand grabs Hamlet by the throat and slams him to a tree.

- A series of **flashbacks** illustrate and explain the Ghost's long speeches about his marriage to Gertrude and about his brother.

- Graphic **extreme close-up shots** dramatize the effects of the poison and the extreme horror of King Hamlet's death.

- A troubling disconnect is suggested between King Hamlet's affection for his wife and son and the Ghost's cold menace.

- A series of **separation shots in medium, close-up, and extreme close-up** tends to humanize Hamlet and dehumanize the Ghost (extreme close-ups of the Ghost's gas-jet-blue eyes make him look "like a predator or an animal," one student said).

- A final, **over-the-shoulder shot** in which the armored glove of the Ghost reaches down to touch Hamlet's ungloved hand is punctuated by a ghostly **fade** that conveys failed contact.

What story about a son, a ghost, and a father do the camera, editing, and sound tell in Branagh's adaptation? Students see and hear the aftermath of violence in a powerful and dysfunctional family; the disconnect between Hamlet and the Ghost in this production causes students to question whether indeed the Ghost is Hamlet's father, a demon, or some phantasmagoric figure of Hamlet's twisted imagination.

Hamlet. 2000. Directed by Michael Almereyda. Ethan Hawke as Hamlet, Sam Shepard as Ghost. Director of Photography, John de Borman. DVD Chapter 4.

- **Establishing shots** of a limo in New York City at night with the expected **environmental sounds** are replaced by tense symphonic **music.**

- **Full shots** of Gertrude and Claudius inside a limo embracing **cut** to a **separation medium shot** of Hamlet in the opposite seat, looking away in disgust.

- **Long shots** of the limo pulling up to a celebrity event establish Gertrude and Claudius as a power couple, swamped by the media. In contrast, Hamlet recedes, while all **vocal and environmental sounds** are unnaturally muted and the **music** intensifies.

- A **location** shift to the Hotel Elsinore conveys a fortress-like setting with a **close-up shot** of security monitors, and **medium and long shots** of Hamlet in his apartment sleeping, waking, and seeing through glass walls distorted reflections and the figure of what appears to be an ordinary businessman on his balcony, holding a cloth to one ear.

- At the frame's edge of medium and long shots, **visual details** of objects in Hamlet's apartment include a television with the volume muted, broadcasting hellish images.

- A dramatic combination of **conversation shots**, most in **medium and close-up**, **eye-level**, frames Hamlet and the Ghost. They are often filmed together in **objective two-shots**, the camera **zooming** in slowly to close-ups.

- The camera **pans** in a circle that follows the Ghost's circular movement in the room.

- The Ghost makes repeated physical contact with Hamlet, his intentions unclear—is he threatening Hamlet? Is he trying to protect him?
- The Ghost's **voice** cracks when he names Hamlet's mother; Hamlet grabs for air when the Ghost releases him from his parting embrace.

What story does this camera work, editing, and sound design tell about the royal house of Denmark Corporation? Students think that the disconnect this camera emphasizes is not so much between son and father as between son and mother, but they aren't sure about this Ghost's purposes; one student commented that circles are symbols of unity, but when the Ghost and the camera circle Hamlet's room, "it looks like he's being stalked." In spite of the fact that Hamlet and the Ghost appear together in so many objective full shots, this usually causes students to see their differences more starkly than their similarities—"He's not like his father"—and students aren't sure about this son's ability to carry out revenge. Still, in comparison to the Branagh clip, my students almost always feel greater empathy with this young Hamlet and his business-suited Ghost.

> *Hamlet*. 1990. Directed by Franco Zeffirelli. Mel Gibson as Hamlet, Paul Scofield as Ghost. Director of Photography, David Watkin. DVD Chapters 7 and 8.

- The **location** is a maze-like castle with multiple stone stairways, corridors, archways, and (I usually have to tell students this word) a battlement at the top with notched stonework overlooking the sea.
- The **lighting**—these film sequences are so dark and shadowy that if the classroom window shades are not fully drawn, students barely see the Ghost in long shots.
- Before seeing the Ghost, a **low-angle camera** looks up at Hamlet looking down at a brightly lit banquet; in an **overhead shot,** the camera looks down on the banquet.
- The **sound** design is carefully layered: **environmental** sounds include the scraping of boots on stone walkways and wind; separate from the spare orchestral **music**, students detect an odd, high-pitched **sound effect** they think expresses the presence of the supernatural.
- The first shot of the Ghost is a **close-up** of an old, unarmed man, dressed not in armor or a suit but in a simple robe that looks almost religious.
- At the top of the battlements, the camera **pans** the location even as Hamlet does, nervously looking for the Ghost.

- Hamlet and the Ghost are almost always filmed in subjective **separation shots**; they appear together in only one objective full shot, and it is a **long shot** with distance between them (actually, there is a second, brief shot in which the camera shows the ghost at mid-range and part of Hamlet's body in the foreground).

- During their conversation there are many **separate, eye-line-match shots** of Hamlet and the Ghost, with **close-up shots** of Hamlet's emotional face and **close-up or medium shots** of the Ghost.

- The camera often **zooms** in slowly in separation **close-up shots** of Hamlet and the Ghost.

- In a **close-up shot,** the camera slowly **zooms** on a **visual detail** of the Ghost's face, one tear dropping from the Ghost's eye.

- A **final shot** in which the Ghost's hands reach slowly toward Hamlet as if to hold him one last time cuts to a **reverse shot** of Hamlet, his own hands raised with the shadow of ghostly hands on his face, but either the Ghost disappears before he can touch his son or his hands **fade** to shadows. Either way, Hamlet raises his hands to emptiness, never making physical contact with the Ghost.

What story about a son, a ghost, and a father do the camera, editing, and sound tell in Zeffirelli's story? Even this Hamlet, the "bravest Hamlet" students have seen today, looks overwhelmed and broken by sorrow for a gentle, saint-like father separated from his son not only by death but also by a camera that almost refuses to let them share the same frame. The cinematic techniques used to develop the mood, the relationship, and the conflict Hamlet inherits in this production emphasize a terrible loss.

Play-by-Play

When English and film studies teacher Josh H. Cabat wanted students to talk the talk of Shakespeare on film, he created a project he calls "Yak Traks," in which students use ripping programs to download a scene from a play they have read, load it into iMovie, remove the audio track, and speak their own play-by-play analysis into computer microphones, commenting on the most surprising and significant directorial choices they see and hear. Prompting students with variations of the question "What do you notice now?," Cabat and his students record voice-overs that provide fresh, informal, and informed analyses of the theatrical choices in the scene, from entrances and exits to lighting, costumes, line delivery, action, and gesture, but he also prompts them to comment on such cinematic devices as lighting and camera shots. Students not only comment on how a film clip recomposes the scene they have read but also postulate on the why.

One student who worked with the 2008 PBS production of *King Lear* directed by Trevor Nunn notes that in the film's opening shot sequence, Ian McKellan in the role of Lear enters a dark set illuminated by a beam of light "that reflects the dark themes of the play." The student describes Lear's costume as "clergy-ware" and his gestures and movements in what "almost looks like a religious ritual," with Lear performing "some sort of blessing." These immediate choices establish "the level of respect with which he is treated" before the play begins. This project readily lends itself to cinematic analysis with the addition of Handout 5.1, "Seeing the Unexpected," used as a guide to student commentary. Cabat describes Yak Trak and other fascinating multimodal projects in his *English Journal* article, "'The Lash of Film': New Paradigms of Visuality in Teaching Shakespeare" (56–57).

Amid the confusion of newly made lesson plans on audio and video Shakespeare that we lug into the classroom on a weekly basis, we can take comfort in the words of Oscar-winning cinematographer Gregg Toland, who explained when he offered to shoot *Citizen Kane* (1941) for the young Orson Welles, a man who had never before directed a film, "I want to work with somebody who never made a movie. That's the only way to learn anything—from somebody who doesn't know anything" (Barsam and Monahan 209). There are no professional directors or film scholars in the secondary classroom, just teachers and students who can learn from one another how to see the ghost of cinematic language and the spirit, if not the letter, of Shakespeare on film.

6 Reading, Reconnected

Your face, my thane, is as a book where men
May read strange matters.

Macbeth 1.5.73–74

We do not eject books each time we insert a DVD in the Shakespeare classroom; they are paper and digital sheaves of the same text writ large. Film returns us to our books, bilingual.

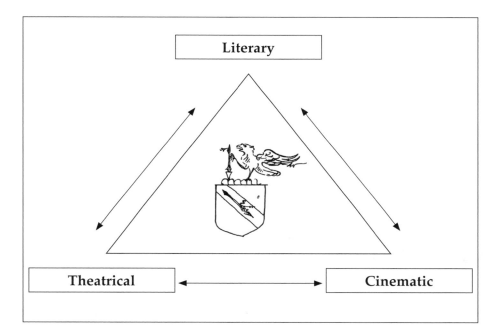

Once we learn to speak the basic language of cinematic composition and to read Shakespeare recomposed on film, we arrive back at the apex of Shakespeare's triangle better equipped to imagine the visual, symbolic, connotative, and auditory possibilities of Shakespeare's language and to analyze the rhetorical complexities of narrative. We return to Hamlet's "To be or not to be" soliloquy for the words that inspired director Michael Almereyda to locate it among the action flicks in a Blockbuster video store; we generate character traits for the Lady Macbeth we meet in act 1, scene 5, view film interpretations for their contradictory theatrical and cinematic readings, and add more traits to our list; we debate the moral ambiguity of Henry V's victory at Agincourt, listen for the ways in which Olivier's sound track, in its line cuts, vocal tones, music, and sound effects, argues unambiguously for glory, and then return to the text in act 4 with a directorial pen, deleting lines that contradict our own reading of Henry's battle.

In retrospect, I should have known that the natural inclination of film in the English classroom is to return us home again to the literary, but it wasn't until I incorporated documentaries into the Shakespeare class that I fully appreciated the primacy of characters, setting, plot, language, and theme in all of the stories we tell. After looking at them in the less-familiar context of film, the familiar elements of storytelling suffer a sea change into something truly rich and strange.

Looking for Shakespeare behind Bars

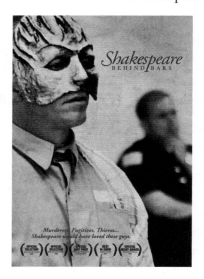

In conjunction with our word-first reading of *The Tempest* and the 2010 film trailer it inspired (see Chapter 2), I decided to give our Fridays in the Shakespeare class to the focused viewing of clips from Hank Rogerson's 2005 documentary, *Shakespeare behind Bars*, a film whose title names the organization that, through performance, creatively confronts the incarcerated with William Shakespeare, with personal and social issues, and with themselves. My purpose was practical: the film chronicles rehearsal sessions for a performance of *The Tempest* inside Kentucky's Luther Luckett prison, so we would see and hear parts of the play we were reading, and in our word-first reading of Shakespeare's play I worried that without periodic practice, students might not retain their emerging knowledge of Shakespeare on film. Still, I doubted: how, if at all, could a film spoken largely in language that is neither Shakespeare's nor a screenwriter's, by speakers who are not actors but actual people identically dressed, challenge us with its literary and theatrical elements? And as for the cinematic, I simply didn't associate documentary films with cinematic style; things just happen and you film them, right?

By the second Friday, I knew how wrong I was. After our first viewing, students expressed such emotional involvement in the world of the film that I realized a documentary is just as powerful as any of the fictional film clips we had viewed and perhaps more so because, at its best, the documentary film genre pursues truth in both objective and subjective ways. *Do these inmates deserve our sympathy,* the director seemed to ask, *and can speaking Shakespeare change lives?* Perhaps influenced by some of the personal and social dysfunction in their own families, students could not agree on answers to these and other questions that sprang haphazardly from our first viewing.

In preparation for the second viewing, I revised and reformatted the question sets on the three faces of film (Handout 3.2) into a focused viewing chart, Handout 6.1, and asked students to focus on one of the three faces. After watching the second film clip only once, students wrote their observations in the second column and then met in homogeneous focus groups to share their observations. Based on past viewings of Shakespeare films, I had assumed that only a few students would choose to focus on the literary face, but again I was wrong. No matter which of the three faces they focused on, students were reading the story of the film first and recognizing the theatrical and cinematic details second. Our summary conversation was a necessary act of synthesis.

Displaying the essential questions that had sprung from our first viewing—"Do these inmates deserve our sympathy? Can speaking Shakespeare change lives?"—I asked students to look to their focused notes for answers. Even students who had focused on the theatrical and the cinematic elements of the film were organically connecting their observations of acting, set, photography, and sound to our questions about the characters, conflicts, issues, and ideas.

Students saw the prison and its geographic location not only as the setting but also as a symbol of "everything wild and isolated, like Prospero's island." They noted that exterior shots of the prison, the wide-open, barren terrain, and low-angle shots of the sky with clouds moving in fast-motion photography "contribute irony to the closed-in world of prison." One student asked a question essential to the genre: "Can people in a documentary be considered characters and actors?" Students continued to debate the character traits of the inmates—some students called them "sad, thoughtful, remorseful," others called them "hopeful of a second chance," and one student called them "manipulative, only showing us their good side"—which, I suggested, indicates that these men are not static but dynamic and capable of change.

Students made an interesting discovery about language and vocal sound in this film: "There's some music but almost all of the sound is the human voice talking and speaking," Kannika read from her notes.

"The only shouting seems limited to Shakespeare's dialogue." Students agreed that this was uncharacteristic of their notions of violent criminals and unexpected in the setting of a medium-security prison for men. "Can speaking Shakespeare change lives?" I asked again, redirecting students' attention to our second essential question. "Is speaking Shakespeare a way to channel our most intense emotions?" So many of the students who had focused on the literary ("Write down one great line!") had recorded the same sentence spoken by one of the inmates in a thoughtful, matter-of-fact tone—"Not talking got me here"—that we agreed we had discovered, literally in the voice of the film, not only a provocative answer to one of our questions but also a theme central to Rogerson's film. Our classroom conversation was confirmed a year later as I read *Shakespeare Inside: The Bard behind Bars*, a nonfiction account of the people and events filmed in this documentary; author Amy Scott-Douglass grounds the cinematic elements of the film in the literary depths of language and the human experience.

Encouraged to continue looking at the literary familiar in the cinematic less familiar (i.e., the text of not-quite-Shakespeare-on-film films about Shakespeare), I added clips from Al Pacino's 1996 hybrid documentary, *Looking for Richard,* to our Friday viewings. Hearkening to the centrality of the rhetorical triangle (Figure 1.2) in the Advanced Placement English language course, I wanted students in the open-enrollment Shakespeare elective, some of whom actually fail English 11 or 12, to grapple with the word at the center of the triangle, *purpose,* an element that controls almost every choice a composer makes. In his film, Pacino makes it immediately clear that his purpose is to get at answers to a question essential to a Shakespeare actor and his American audience: "What gets between us and Shakespeare?" But I had a few questions of my own, and I suspected that an exploration of the purposes of filmmakers such as Hank Rogerson and Al Pacino would guide us to a closer understanding of the power of stories and art to bring us together and make us whole.

After we viewed the second of two clips of Pacino's film guided by Handout 6.1, I projected posters of the two documentaries onto the SMART Board and asked, "What is the purpose of each of these documentary films? Generate a list of filmmakers' purposes." The first response was "to entertain." I agreed that this was a general purpose of most filmmakers and many composers of all types of text, adding some other broad, foundational purposes: to narrate, to explain, to analyze, to persuade. Then I asked students to be more specific: "If we could talk to each director right now and ask him what he most wanted to accomplish in his film, what would Rogerson say? What would Pacino say?" Speaking about *Shakespeare behind Bars*, Aaron said that Rogerson's purpose is to show that Shakespeare belongs in prisons too, that "his plays have no boundaries" and can be performed by everyone. Speaking about *Looking for Richard*, Javier struggled to recall the words of a homeless man interviewed in Pacino's film and then attempted a paraphrase: "Pacino wants to show that Shakespeare belongs to the people, not just actors and experts." Finally, I displayed a purpose statement by director Stanley Kubrick (qtd. in Theodosakis 93):

> "[T]he basic purpose of a film . . . is one of illumination, of showing the viewer something he can't see any other way."

To illuminate is "to brighten, to make understandable, to expose" (*American Heritage Dictionary*). I knew that in the weeks to come, I would ask students to plan, produce, and illuminate their own quest for understanding within the genre of the documentary (see Chapter 8), but for now we had taken a series of important first steps.

The Play within the Story within the Film

Since I first began to teach the Shakespeare elective in 2001, John Madden's 1998 *Shakespeare in Love* has been a part of the course, at first as an end-of-semester celebration and a way to alleviate the pressure of semester exams. But when our school purchased a class set of Marc Norman and Tom Stoppard's screenplay, I went to work on a series of reading and viewing lesson plans and moved *Shakespeare in Love* away from the final exam schedule. Since the film is a fictional account of young Will Shakespeare's writing of *Romeo and Juliet*, I constructed a prereading plot chart, Figure 6.1, and chunked the text of the screenplay into four readings:

> **First Reading**: Pages 1–45, ending at "VIOLA'S eyes are searching the room for WILL. She finds WESSEX smiling at her. She looks away."
>
> **Second Reading**: Pages 46–67, ending at "But WILL has gone."
>
> **Third Reading**: Pages 68–116, ending at "The words of the scene become WILL'S and VIOLA'S, their way of saying the farewells they cannot utter."
>
> **Fourth Reading**: Pages 116–end.

Romeo and Juliet | Shakespeare in Love | Twelfth Night
Points of Intersection

Romeo and Juliet	Shakespeare in Love
Act 1.3: Lady Capulet encourages marriage.	p. 37: Lady DeLesseps encourages marriage.
1.5: The Capulets' banquet	p. 41: The DeLessups' banquet
1.2: Paris and Capulet bargain over Juliet.	p. 42: Wessex and Sir Robert bargain over Viola.
2.2: Juliet's balcony	p. 45: Viola's balcony p. 78: The players rehearse.
1.1: Lovesick Romeo confides in Benvolio.	p. 55: The players begin to rehearse.
4.2: Juliet "submits" to her father and agrees to marry Paris.	p. 59: Viola submits to her father and will marry Wessex.
2.1: Blind love, blind Romeo	p. 64–67: Will discovers his own "blindness"—Thomas's true identity.
3.5: Romeo and Juliet consummate their marriage and then bid each other farewell.	p. 68: Viola and Will consummate their relationship. p. 116: Will and Viola read 3.5 in bed and speak their own farewells.
3.1: Capulets and Montagues fight, Tybalt versus Mercutio.	p. 98–102: The Chamberlain's Men fight the Admiral's Men, Burbage versus Alleyn.
3.1: Mercutio is dead! Romeo feels responsible.	p. 107: Marlowe is dead! Will feels responsible.
5.3: Juliet wakes in the tomb to find Romeo dead.	p. 108–13: Viola thinks Will is dead and mourns him. Will is not dead. p. 114: Will has written act 5, scene 3—Juliet and Romeo will die.
Twelfth Night	Viola is shipwrecked off the coast of the New World. . . .

Figure 6.1. Prereading plot chart for *Romeo and Juliet* and *Shakespeare in Love*.

Still, in the first few years each active reading lesson was followed by a passive viewing of clips from the film. Then in 2008 I read a book about media literacy in the English classroom cowritten by Mary T. Christel, who declares that film in the literature class can and should be much more than "the dessert after a multicourse repast of reading, writing, and testing" (Krueger and Christel 68). Inspired and guided by the groundbreaking work of Ellen Krueger and Christel and Alan B. Teasley and Ann Wilder, I began to develop active viewing guides that eventually became Shakespeare's triangle, Handouts 3.6 and 5.4, and the focused viewing chart, Handout 6.1, and we used these in various combinations each time we shifted from Norman and Stoppard's screenplay to Madden's film.

But recently, in the course of researching and writing a book that walks the distance between three points on a triangle from literary to theatrical and cinematic, I reread John Golden's 2007 *English Journal* article, "Literature into Film (and Back Again)," and remembered there is a fourth point on the triangle, a literary home plate where, "at the end of all our exploring," as T. S. Eliot writes, we will "arrive where we started, And know the place for the first time" (59). "How does the director," Golden asks his students as he asks us all, "use cinematic and theatrical elements to illustrate literary elements?" ("Literature" 25). In the focused viewing of Shakespeare film clips that my students and I had been doing with increasing regularity, we were almost always making connections between the three points, but at times the focus felt bottom-heavy. Golden's question brought us home.

Somewhere between the first and third screenplay readings, I constructed the first draft of a new viewing guide, one that highlights the literary in literature and film. Building on viewing notes of the Nurse (played by Imelda Staunton) written by a student after our first reading, I prepared an example of the work I hoped students could do together (Handout 6.2) and then lugged a newly revised lesson plan into the classroom, one that ends with questions inspired by Golden's article: "How does the film translate your character? What is lost and gained in translation?"

Perhaps because we were reading a screenplay and the film it engendered, most students felt that their readings of a character were not so much changed as intensified by the acting and camera work. Student Steven Crowe read Will in the screenplay as "torn between Will the writer, Will the lover, and Will the commoner of Stratford-upon-Avon and husband of another woman." The Will who is "torn" in Steven's reading becomes "a split personality" in the film's camera work: "In almost every shot, Will's face is divided into a light and a dark side. The only time his face is directly lit is when he is with Viola, at the riverside and in her bed." The language of Norman and Stoppard's screenplay is enriched with literary wordplay, and this is one example of a student's growing ability to see the cinesthetic translation of literature's aesthetic language.

Back to the Books

Reading literature closely enough to construct an understanding of the characters, conflict, rhetorical and aesthetic language, tone, mood, and themes constitutes first sight in the English classroom; identifying theatrical and cinematic elements in a film production of that passage in one or two viewings requires second sight; third sight is the ability to reconnect graphic and moving images and nonverbal sound to the elements of language and literature. As we continued to channel observations of the theatrical and the cinematic in a Shakespeare film clip back to the literary source, the classroom dynamic changed. Every reader of Shakespeare is a struggling reader, but some of the least confident students in the Shakespeare class—students on academic probation, mainstreamed English language learners, students with learning disabilities and modified instructional plans—began to take a more active part in our whole-group discussions of Shakespeare's literary text.

In his introduction to *Reading in the Dark*, Golden wonders if we haven't got it backwards, if focusing first on the literary elements of film and *then* on literature itself might be a better way to engage reluctant readers in the kind of critical analyses of text that all students are expected to engage in. Golden arrived at this theory after first teaching a five-week unit on film in a senior English course, followed by a unit on the novel. He noticed that "the watching and analyzing of movies seemed to greatly affect [students'] ability to read and critique literature" (xiv). In the same serendipitous spirit, colleague and English teacher Althea Terenzi discovered as she worked with two sections of sophomores that sometimes the better way to analyze literary Shakespeare is to read from the base of the triangle.

After sending colleagues a blank template of the "Focus on Literature" viewing chart (Handout 6.3), I heard immediately from Terenzi, whose students had just read act 2, scenes 2 and 3 of *Macbeth*, scenes that dramatize Macbeth's horror at what he has done to his king, and the discovery of Duncan's body. Though they were not as practiced at reading Shakespeare on film as were students in the Shakespeare elective, Terenzi's students had been introduced to the glossary of film terms (Handout 3.1) and the concept of Shakespeare's three faces. "My students are not overly fond of handouts, especially if they are very complex," she explained, so she modified the lesson with the addition of large sheets of paper, a T-chart, and sticky notes.

With the focus on characterization, students worked in small groups of two or three on a single character, watching the film clip from the 2010 production of *Macbeth* directed by Rupert Goold and writing their observations of their character's actions, gestures, facial expressions, and line delivery as well as of costumes, set, camera work, and sound on sticky notes.

After viewing, they pooled their notes, omitting repeats, and attached the sticky notes to the appropriate column on the larger paper, which had been divided into a T-chart for theatrical elements and cinematic elements.

To get students to the next step, connecting the theatrical and the cinematic elements to characterization, Terenzi asked them to go back to each sticky, lift each as if it were a flap, and write under the flap how that theatrical or cinematic element helps to characterize the person. "Writing short notes on small pieces of paper might trick them into thinking they're not writing very much," Terenzi observed, "whereas the worksheet might seem more daunting at first." About two weeks later, when her students had read act 3, scene 4, the scene in which the bloody ghost of Banquo appears at Macbeth's feast, Terenzi believed they were ready to tackle the challenge of focused viewing using the handout. This is an outline of her lesson plan:

1. Display four film stills of the three witches from various performances. Students complete this sentence for each one: "These witches seem _____ because _____."

2. Briefly review act 3, scene 4 aloud. Distribute blank templates of Handout 6.2. Students complete the first chart (Literary) on their own after selecting a character (Macbeth, Lady Macbeth, Ghost of Banquo, etc.). Circulate to see their work.

3. After reviewing the directions and discussing the basics of theatrical (acting, costumes, makeup, props) and cinematic (camera work, editing, location, lighting, sound) elements, we view the Goold production of 3.4. Students take notes as they watch. Circulate to see their work.

4. In the last ten minutes of class, students share their observations and I ask them questions about why these elements were added to the film and what they reveal about a character.

During and after the viewing, Terenzi's students had many questions pertaining to which column of Figure 6.2 they should put their notes, the "theatrical" or the "cinematic," and though they were good at noting details while they viewed, they were unsure about how to interpret them. Only a few students were able to use the handout to organize their observations and interpret how a particular element contributes to characterization; one student wrote in the Theatrical column that Patrick Stewart has a mustache "so he'd remind us of Hitler."

Theatrical	Cinematic
How do the <u>actors</u> (line delivery, facial expressions, actions and gestures) illustrate the literary element of characterization? How do the costumes, makeup, and props help?	How does the <u>director</u> illustrate the literary element of characterization? How do the camera work (shots, angles, focus, movement), editing, location, lighting, and sound (vocal, environmental, music, silence) help?

Figure 6.2. Theatrical versus cinematic elements chart.

"Perhaps if we had done a separate lesson with the objective of just identifying an element as theatrical or cinematic, this would not have been a problem," Terenzi said, "but as it was, this seemed to be a distraction, since my main objective was to focus on characterization." Terenzi's take-away was to combine the theatrical and the cinematic into one column and leave the other column as a space for interpreting and connecting, either during or after viewing. Handout 6.3 combines the work of a teacher who has more opportunities to explore reading Shakespeare on film with the work of a teacher who has less. The hand-out works in both classrooms.

At the same time that Terenzi was modifying and adding to the work of reading *Macbeth* as both text and film, colleague Matthew Despres wanted students to synthesize what they were learning about the how and why of film characterization, so he added a writing component. Seeing the character of Lady Macbeth as a rich and rare opportunity for students to focus on a complex female character in literature, Despres chose act 5, scene 1, the sleepwalking scene, as the subject of comparative analysis. After their reading of the scene, most of Despres's students had characterized Lady Macbeth as both "cruel" and "anxious," so he used their own words to focus their viewing of two productions. "How do the filmmakers and actors illustrate cruelty and anxiety?" he asked his students. "What do they do with visuals and sound that Shakespeare accomplishes with words alone?"

Student Maria Zahir saw in the 1971 Roman Polanski production a Lady Macbeth, performed by Francesca Annis, who no longer lives in her "comfortable" world of Dunsinane Castle but is forced by her own mind to wander inside a cruel, strange place. She now sleepwalks, "nude . . . as a newborn," drawn to "the simple safe light" of a candle at her writing desk, the velvet curtains near her bed, and her Doctor's sleeve, as temporary "comfort zones." She speaks in "tones of misery and despair," and "the camera captures the strain in her neck, and the tightness of her jaw. It insists upon the medium shot . . . and when Lady Macbeth pleads goodnight, the camera does not follow," refusing in its distance to get too close to a woman whose cruelty once encompassed the capacity to kill. "Moving around inside her head," Maria concludes, "is something naked that sleeps until sure it is alone." What Polanski does with visuals and sound in this production is to convey the effects of cruelty in an actor's tortured anxiety.

After we arrive back at the beginning, the apex of Shakespeare's triangle, how has our study of the language of film contributed to our comprehension of the myriad symbols and signs of human expression? One way to find out is to take a second trip around the triangle.

Reading Shakespeare in Triplicate

Our road map is Handout 6.4; from there, though I offer suggestions about possible text-and-film pairings, students decide which speech or scene from which play they want to focus on, even down to whether we will work on individual pairings or together as a class with a single, shared Shakespeare passage and film. When I offered these choices to students in 2011, they agreed that we work better as a team, and even though we do not read *Romeo and Juliet* in the Shakespeare elective, their work with Madden's *Shakespeare in Love* prompted them to choose act 5, scene 3 from Shakespeare's play and the final scene from Luhrmann's 1996 cultural adaptation, *Romeo + Juliet*. To alleviate the stress of plot, I reformatted the Folger summary of *Romeo and Juliet* 5.3 into a plotline, Figure 6.3. Directors often delete events or rearrange the sequence of events in a Shakespeare play, and a plotline can help students note the changes.

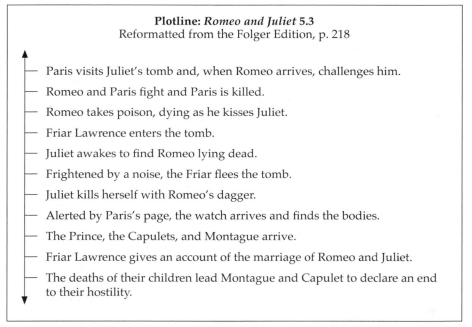

Plotline: *Romeo and Juliet* 5.3
Reformatted from the Folger Edition, p. 218

— Paris visits Juliet's tomb and, when Romeo arrives, challenges him.

— Romeo and Paris fight and Paris is killed.

— Romeo takes poison, dying as he kisses Juliet.

— Friar Lawrence enters the tomb.

— Juliet awakes to find Romeo lying dead.

— Frightened by a noise, the Friar flees the tomb.

— Juliet kills herself with Romeo's dagger.

— Alerted by Paris's page, the watch arrives and finds the bodies.

— The Prince, the Capulets, and Montague arrive.

— Friar Lawrence gives an account of the marriage of Romeo and Juliet.

— The deaths of their children lead Montague and Capulet to declare an end to their hostility.

Figure 6.3. Plotline of *Romeo and Juliet*.

If students are working with a passage they have already read, chunked, annotated, and/or analyzed in Shakespeare literature circles (see Chapters 6–9 in *Reading Shakespeare with Young Adults* [Dakin]), you might be able to assign an independent rereading and move ahead to the screenplay or film. Since we had chosen a scene from a play that some but not all students had read in grade 8 English class, I distributed copies of act 5, scene 3 and redistributed laminated copies of the "Annotating Shakespeare" bookmark (Figure 7.2 in *Reading Shakespeare with Young Adults* [Dakin]). Then I projected Shakespeare's triangle to guide our first reading:

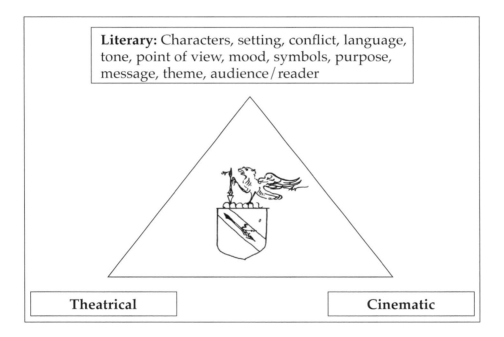

Literary: Characters, setting, conflict, language, tone, point of view, mood, symbols, purpose, message, theme, audience/reader

Theatrical

Cinematic

There is so much happening on a single page of Shakespeare's text that no reader can take it all in during a first or second reading, but the bookmark is a helpful reminder of where to look for answers to the questions we all have as we read Shakespeare.

After reading the passage together or in literature circles, the next act is to think like a twenty-first-century filmmaker. With their copies of act 5, scene 3 in hand, students slashed the script, deleting words, sentences, and even characters, keeping only what they considered most essential. The challenge of "Act 3" (Handout 6.4 is still our guide) is to put it all back again, in the form of directorial commentary written in the margins or on sticky notes. Although the question once sounded like sin to this reader's ear, I ask it boldly now: "What theatrical and cinematic language can replace the words of Shakespeare's text?" With every attempt at an answer, students learn to converse with text in multilingual tongues.

The fourth act depends on the resources and time at hand. My students were able to download, free of charge, the screenplay for *Romeo + Juliet* written by Craig Pearce and Baz Luhrmann; we read from page 102, "EXT. CEMETERY. NIGHT. CLOSE ON: A stone angel etched against the night sky . . ." to the end of the screenplay before viewing the film. If they have access to the screenplay, students can even read comparatively, crossing out what the director and writer crossed out, and wondering at what the deletions, inclusions, and interpolations reveal about the director's purpose and the message. In her examination of the radical changes to the final scene in the Folio text of *Romeo and Juliet* made by director Luhrmann, who "cuts both Paris and the [paternal] Friar . . . and allows the innocent Romeo to see Juliet alive the moment after he has drunk the fatal poison," Deborah Cartmell concludes that this pair of star-crossed lovers is "more mature and therefore more responsible for their fate," yet fated to be born into a world constrained not by sexuality but by violence (43–47). The main event in "Act 4" is to view the film clip twice, focusing first on the theatrical point of the triangle (Handout 3.6) and then on the cinematic (Handout 5.4).

Finally, we return to the literary apex of the triangle, and students engage in a full examination of the transmediation of Shakespeare's text, responding in writing or in an oral presentation to John Golden's great question about the act of translating "Literature into Film (and Back Again)": "How does the director use cinematic and theatrical elements to illustrate literary elements?" (25).

"In *Romeo + Juliet*," student Jordan Rodriguez begins, "elements of the play are lost and regained." Lillian McKinley quantifies the loss: "Out of the Folger's 321 lines, only 58 lines remain in the screenplay, or 18%," yet she argues that the body language and vocals of the actors, the set, props, lighting, and music put back in what is lost. "Juliet's last lines are also missing," she admits, but "while this is partially to allow for the change in prop—a gun instead of a dagger—the seconds of silence before the gunshot seem more powerful than lines." In spite of the intensity and complexity of the sound design in this scene (police sirens, helicopters, a solo soprano, orchestral music, breathing, crying, speaking), Xuyen Mai comments that "the silence in this scene is suffocating."

Students repeatedly commented on the prop of Romeo's gun and the extent to which it contrasts with the neon crosses, vigil candles, religious statues, and flowers in the scene. "Juliet is holding a white lily, symbol of peace and eternal life," Lillian writes. "Into the midst of this, Romeo lays down a gun, symbol of death and violence." Lindsay Chorlian sees the placement of a lone gun among the lilies and candles as the director's use of "foreshadowing to Romeo that life is more powerful than death and that Juliet is still alive although she appears dead," a hint that Romeo tragically fails to take. "The most powerful antithesis," Lillian writes, "comes at Juliet's death, when her red blood spills on her white dress. At the end, she is again wrapped in white, this time, a sheet as she is taken from the scene."

In the course of our study of Shakespeare on film, my students had viewed only the opening and closing sequences of Baz Luhrmann's film, yet they were repeatedly surprised by the recurrent religious images that haunt the film. "Act 5.3 takes place in a cemetery and a tomb," Jordan writes, "but Luhrmann puts it in a church . . . and the scene starts with long shots and close up shots of a statue of Jesus Christ." Though in their writing no student elevated the religious imagery in Lurhmann's film to the level of director's purpose or film's message, Marissa Maccioli made a remarkable connection between the world of Shakespeare's play and Luhrmann's perception of our own: "Deeply embedded in this film," she writes, "is the role of religion in a violent world. Unlike in the play, the vault where Juliet's body rests is not seen as a monster that has devoured her but a refuge and safe house for angels." Still, at the end of the conversation shot sequence between the dying Romeo and the grief-stunned Juliet, Xuyen believes that not even God in this film is spared from blame: "The most memorable shot is the overhead full shot that zooms out from Juliet and Romeo, with the focus on Juliet shooting herself with a gun. She looks straight into the camera above her, as if she is blaming a higher power that made them star-crossed lovers."

In the end, every student but one echoed Jordan's opening statement that what is lost when Shakespeare's poetry is translated into film is regained with images and sound, and each of the students who worked on this project in 2011 found vivid examples of theatrical and cinematic brilliance to support their claim. But one student ended on a different note. Recalling that director Stanley Kubrick sees film's purpose as "one of illumination," student Steven Crowe sees literature's purpose as one of imagination:

> In hindsight, stating what is gained by screenplays and movies is a lot more simple than saying what is lost. The things lost

seem simple and are specific to a book—the feel of a page in your hands, being able to formulate your own vision of characters and events. Shakespeare's text is what directors and screenplay writers use to breathe life into Shakespeare. By reading Shakespeare you enter a world that is suggested by Shakespeare's words but created by you. Although your reading doesn't have the theatrical and cinematic flash of a film, it adds a fourth dimension to Shakespeare's triangle—yours, mine. The reason that Shakespeare has stood the test of time is that amazing things always happen when Shakespeare and a reader's imagination collide.

When a filmmaker translates the literary elements of a passage from Shakespeare using theatrical and cinematic elements, what *is* lost and gained in translation? Gazing at this question in a close-up shot with the school calendar at eye level, I know that classroom time for reading Shakespeare on the page is lost. And if we use film in the Shakespeare unit to show students, borrowing from Kubrick, "something [they] can't see any other way," Steven's point is that they can. But great film adaptations of Shakespeare are not merely derivatives of literature; the relationship between text and film is symbiotic. The things we gain when we crosscut from the page to the screen and back again include a greater understanding of the tools of translation, a cinematic vocabulary and an ability to read the diction of film phrases and the paragraph-like syntax of a shot sequence, a keener awareness of the emotional and psychological appeals of cinematic composition, and an eye for cinematic metaphors. Furthermore, we acquire an ear for sound that brings us back in time to an Elizabethan theater and an audience that looks upon a stage so bare that it requires of us everything we have to listen, to imagine, to wonder, and to learn.

7 Reading Shakespeare in Full-Length Films

O, for a muse of fire that would ascend
The brightest heaven of invention!
A kingdom for a stage, princes to act,
And monarchs to behold the swelling scene!

Henry V, Prologue

There is a fascinating detail in the opening scene of Laurence Olivier's epic 1944 film production of *Henry V* that is easy to miss. After the camera pans across the model of Shakespeare's London and zooms to the Globe Theatre where the Lord Chamberlain's Men are about to begin the play, an actor in the role of William Shakespeare plays line prompter to the company. Dressed in Elizabethan garments, Will wears an anachronistic pair of modern eyeglasses. Could this be a costume oversight? Ron Rosenbaum, author of *The Shakespeare Wars*, thinks not. "It is Olivier's sly way of proposing" that he is showing us "the text as Shakespeare himself would have seen it through twentieth century *lenses*, which of course," Rosenbaum concludes, "are the lenses of the motion picture camera" (336).

Viewing an entire film in the Shakespeare course or as the Shakespeare unit in a literature or film course provides students with an extended opportunity not only to practice critical media literacy skills but also to witness the collaboration of genius that is recorded in the best Shakespeare films and to explore the nature and source of that genius.

What? When? How?

What full-length film we show can be a film adaptation of the play our students have just read, spoken in Shakespeare's language and set in a historical period other than the one in which the film was produced—for example, Franco Zeffirelli's 1990 *Hamlet*. We can show a cross-cultural adaptation of the play, spoken in a foreign language with subtitles—for example, Akira Kurosawa's 1957 *Macbeth* adaptation, *Throne of Blood*. We can show a contemporary update of the play, spoken in Shakespeare's language but translated into modern culture—for example, Baz Luhrmann's *Romeo + Juliet*. We can show an offshoot (also called a spin-off) film of the play, spoken in modern American dialect and set in the present of the film's production—for example, Tim Blake Nelson's 2001 *Othello* off-shoot, *O*. To quantify the choices we have and to help us decide which Shakespeare film to choose, consult Michael LoMonico's *The Shakespeare Book of Lists*. In Chapter 8, LoMonico compiles every conceivable type of Shakespeare film, from silent Shakespeare to American and British television productions to films, adaptations, and spin-offs, through the time of his book's publication in 2001. Most titles are accompanied by helpful annotations.

As if there weren't enough choices, there is also this choice: we can show a Shakespeare film of a play our students have not and will not read in school. The tragedies abound on high school reading lists; consider showing a comedy such as Michael Hoffman's delightful 1999 *A Midsummer Night's Dream*, Branagh's witty 1993 *Much Ado about Nothing*, Trevor Nunn's bittersweet 1996 *Twelfth Night* with Ben Kingsley's haunting musical solos in the role of Feste, or the disturbing 2004 *Merchant of Venice* with Al Pacino in the role of Shylock. As for the histories, there is Richard Loncraine's compelling 1995 update *Richard III*, starring Ian McKellan, Robert Downey Jr., and Annette Bening. My choice for histories is Kenneth Branagh's 1989 *Henry V*, a brilliant cinematic reading of Shakespeare's puzzling play. Finally, Julie Taymor's 2010 production of Shakespeare's romance *The Tempest* can spark debate with its treatment of issues such as gender and race. In the end, the choice of what full-length film we show will depend on our overarching objectives, the needs and interests of students, film availability, and personal preference.

When we show a Shakespeare film will depend on some of the above. I do not recommend showing an entire film of a play before students have read the play, though the argument can be made that showing the whole film functions as a kind of prereading plot summarizer. But unlike graphic maps, Wordle word clouds, and play outlines and summaries, films get inside our heads in ways that can limit and distort our reading; I want students to read Shakespeare with their mind's eye first. So if I choose for whole viewing the film of a play my students are about to read, I am most likely to choose a contemporary update such as Almereyda's *Hamlet* or Luhrmann's *Romeo + Juliet* or an offshoot such as Nelson's *O*. As we read the play, I avoid using clips from this film, and I set aside two weeks of instruction at the end of the play unit for viewing the entire film and engaging in postviewing activities.

How we show a full-length Shakespeare film, or any whole film, is in four or five narrative segments with a viewing guide for each. If we choose a film production of a Shakespeare play that students have read, Figure 6.1 (p. 72) can function as the viewing guide. If we choose a film production of a Shakespeare play that students have *not* read, a film-specific guide will be more helpful. Students will also benefit from the kinds of prereading (now pre*viewing*) strategies described in Chapter 6 of *Reading Shakespeare with Young Adults* [Dakin]: cast lists, summarizers, even a word cloud composed from a play's word-frequency list or a list of key lines from the film they are about to view. Previewing the characters and plot may take most of the first class; then we begin the process of viewing a film segment, taking notes, discussing, and continuing the process tomorrow.

"The single most important tool for teaching film," assert Teasley and Wilder, "is the viewing guide" (52). Their process of constructing viewing guides is summarized here:

1. Teachers preview the film, breaking it into "meaningful chunks" that function like acts or chapters in the movie. Chunks can range from three to forty minutes in length, though the average chunk is about twenty minutes long.

2. Each chunk is the topic of a full-page viewing guide, with space at the top for students' notes and four to five open-ended questions in the lower half of the page that focus student attention on notable aspects of the segment they have just viewed. The questions generally focus attention on the literary, theatrical, and cinematic aspects of the film segment (52–59).

Unless a director and screenwriter have taken liberties with the text, Shakespeare films can be divided into the five acts of the play, though there may be reasons to chunk the film differently. It's worth remembering that Shakespeare did not divide his plays into acts: editors did. In addition to the classic Hollywood three-act model for screenwriting outlined in Chapter 2 of this book, Kristin Thompson argues that most films break into four large-scale, action-packed parts, with high points in the action providing the transitions, or turning points, to the next part. Each part is about twenty to thirty minutes long, catering "to the attention span of the spectator" (43). Her schema, terms, and rationale can be summarized as follows:

1. The setup: A problematical situation is established and the protagonist's goals are established.

2. Complicating action: The situation changes and the protagonist's goals change too. There is clear, gradual character change.

3. Development: There is more change and the protagonist struggles to achieve his or her goals.

4. Climax: Progress toward goals occurs, then resolution. Closure is established (Thompson 27–28, 43).

The decision to chunk a full-length film into three, four, five, or more parts depends on the structure of the film itself and the time constraints of the teaching day.

Handout 7.1, the full-length Shakespeare film viewing guide for director Kenneth Branagh's 1989 adaptation of Shakespeare's history *Henry V* models the construction process developed by Teasley and Wilder. Punctuated by the appearances of Chorus, the structure of Branagh's film easily lends itself to a five-act division, though I decided to cut Chapters 21–26 of the DVD from the act 4 viewing guide because in its entirety, this chunk of the film runs more than fifty minutes.

Postviewing Projects

From writing film reviews to making a film, students should have a variety of opportunities to show what they know about reading Shakespeare on film. The following options offer students a variety of choices.

Critical Film Review

In Appendix 2 of *Great Films and How to Teach Them*, William Costanzo outlines a "Contemporary Film Review" assignment that I have modified for students viewing Shakespeare films. In preparation for their writing, students need to research the film—the director, the actors, and any social or cultural issues surrounding the making of the film. Then we provide them with a framework for writing that can include any combination of these:

A. *Personal Response.* What is your emotional response to the film? What things in the film made the greatest emotional impact on you? What is your intellectual response to the film? What does the film make you think about or question? Will other viewers share your personal response? Why, or why not?

B. *Theatrical Techniques.* If the script is written in Shakespeare's language, what things did the actors do to help you understand the dialogue? How strong is the acting? To what extent do the costumes, makeup, and sets contribute to the effect of the film?

C. *Cinematic Techniques.* What particularly strong (or weak) aspects of the technical elements—camera work, editing, locations and visual details, lighting, sound design—stand out in the film? How do these elements intensify or change the story?

D. *Plot*. Keep this brief. Tell just enough of the story to help the potential film viewer understand it.

E. *Themes*. Shakespeare doesn't tell us what to think; he tells us what to think about (Rosenbaum 349). What ideas and issues does this Shakespeare film challenge us to think about? Make a short list of the abstract nouns that this film explores—love, hate, courage, imagination, justice, power, forgiveness, etc.—and use them as the basis of your comments.

F. *Social Context*. Every artist is influenced by the society in which she or he creates. Research the film—the director, the actors, and any social or cultural issues surrounding the making of the film. Were the actors and the director influenced by social or political movements taking place at the time the film was produced? Is this a film in which Shakespeare's timeless themes are made more timely by social or political events current in our own time?

G. *Contemporary Culture*. How does this Shakespeare film appeal to a modern audience? If the film is set in a culture other than Shakespeare's, what changes have been made and how do those changes enhance or detract from the story?

H. *Rating*. Create a rating system and rate this film using your own scale.

Comparative Analysis

John Golden points out that students need to understand the difference between a movie review and a film analysis ("Literature"). Each has a distinct purpose—the review reacts to a film and seeks to persuade potential viewers to see or not see the film based on this reaction, whereas the analysis seeks to understand and explain the elements of a film.

When students have read the play by William Shakespeare and then viewed the film, they are in a position to write a comparative analysis of the literary and the cinematic texts, but the natural inclination to focus on the changes a director made tends to produce banal results. *Why did the director cut half the lines and eliminate several cast members?* To save time, to make the film less confusing, to make the story better . . . and so on. Through trial and error, Golden has learned that students will write better analyses of the film adaptation when they focus not on the changes made by the director but on the effect of these changes.

"How does the audience feel differently," Golden asks, "about character, theme, plot, and so on because of certain changes that were made?" ("Literature" 27). Using Golden's approach, students prepare to write a film analysis by charting the three different types of change—alterations, deletions, and additions—and the effects of those changes (see Figure 7.1). Students select from their charts four or five significant changes and write analytical essays that focus on the effects, and in essence the effectiveness, of the Shakespeare film adaptation.

Another approach to comparative analysis is suggested by Costanzo and exemplified by Deborah Cartmell in *Interpreting Shakespeare on Screen*. To literally see the ways in which directors reshape Shakespeare's text for film, Cartmell reproduces the Folio text of a key scene and then uses underlining and boldface to show the words the directors kept and the words they cut. In a chapter in which she explores Shakespeare films and the theme of sexuality, we read and see both the extent, and by implication the dramatic effects, of the large-scale editing done by directors Zeffirelli (he retains about 20 percent of the text in the scene) and Luhrmann (he retains only 13 percent) in act 5, scene 3 of *Romeo and Juliet*. The extent of the cuts is shocking to the eye, and Cartmell's analysis of the thematic effects is provocative (53–66). Using her method as an example, we can assign students to select a scene from a Shakespeare film, listen to it as they mark the text of the scene for word and line deletions, and write an essay in which they compare Shakespeare's

Changes—Alterations, Deletions, Additions—between the Print Text of *Hamlet* and the Zeffirelli Film *Hamlet*			
In the Print Text	*Type of Change*	*In the Film*	*Effect of Change*
The character of Fortinbras, Prince of Norway, seeks revenge for his father's death at the hands of King Hamlet.	Deletion	Fortinbras is not in the film. There are no references to him: all the lines that he speaks or that refer to him are cut.	With this external threat to Denmark removed, the internal threats seem greater. And in the end, there is a greater sense of uncertainty because the Danish royal family is dead and only Horatio, a commoner, is left. Who will rule Denmark now?

Figure 7.1. Charting differences between play and film.

script to the director's script, explore the reasons for the changes, and analyze what is lost and gained (Costanzo 176).

A third approach to comparative analysis involves a second film. Whether the Shakespeare film you have selected for class viewing is a classic, such as Max Reinhardt and William Dieterle's 1935 *A Midsummer Night's Dream*, or a remake, like Michael Hoffman's 1999 *Midsummer*, a student interested in film history can view the other film independently and compare the two, focusing the analysis on one or two key scenes (Costanzo 301).

Shot-by-Shot Analysis

A movie is a sequence of still images, called frames, that when viewed in rapid succession create the illusion of the moving picture. Frames compose shots. "A shot," explains William Costanzo, "consists of the frames produced by one continuous operation of the camera" (21). John Golden describes shots as "uninterrupted pieces of film"—uninterrupted, that is, by any editing technique such as a cut, fade, or dissolve. Cuts are like blinks of the eye or split seconds of black. Show students a film clip with the sound off and tell them to clap every time they see these momentary breaks. Students will quickly develop an eye for cinematic grammar (Golden, *Reading* 1–3).

The same rewards that come from closely reading and rereading a play or a poem come from close analysis of a scene in a movie. Although there is no hard-and-fast formula for scene length in a film, many consist of ten to twenty shots. For students who wish to gaze intently at the scene that most captured their attention, Costanzo has developed the shot-by-shot analysis and recommends that it be conducted in teams of two, since collaborative viewing is more likely to yield sharper details and ideas (298). Almost two decades in advance of Costanzo's publication, filmmaker and professor of film at Columbia University Stefan Sharff illustrated his book *The Elements of Cinema* with student-produced shot-by-shot analyses of a shot sequence. Guided by Costanzo and Sharff, I constructed Handout 7.2 and instruct students to address some combination of these elements in writing for each shot:

1. Approximate shot length in seconds
2. Type of camera shot (close-up, medium, long)
3. Camera angle (low angle, high angle, eye level)
4. Any significant camera movement (tilt, crane, zoom, pan, tracking)
5. A brief description of the action, setting, and characters

6. Lighting (high key, low key, back, front, neutral)
7. Sound (key line of dialogue; environmental, music, silence)
8. Transitions (cut, fade, dissolve, wipe, etc.)

After student teams complete the shot-by-shot analysis, they work together or independently on a scene analysis that comments on the ways in which the shots contribute to the conflict, characters, and tone of the scene.

Fan Mail

When Alan B. Teasley and Ann Wilder decided to expand the end products of classroom film viewing, they realized that as their students were analyzing films, they were also analyzing their personal reactions to the characters, situations, and ideas in film. To balance the emphasis on analytical writing with a more personal mode of expression, they developed a new assignment, the letter of reflection. Students explore the connections between themselves and some aspect of the film by writing a letter to their teacher, to the film's director, or to the author of the screenplay. Their letters can be "congratulatory or critical," but as in an analytical essay, they must support their commentary with literary, theatrical, or cinematic evidence. As a third option, they can find a review of the film and write a letter to the film critic in which they agree or disagree with the critic's opinion (67).

Movie Posters

We've all worked with students in the verbal arena of the English classroom whose deepest mode of expression is nonverbal. After Ellen Krueger asked her students to write about "two scenes that left a lingering impression in their minds," she realized that no two viewers see the exact same thing (Krueger and Christel 99). So after the full round of verbal-analytical activities had run their course, she developed an alternative assignment that requires students to design an advertisement commemorating the _____ (number of years) anniversary of _____ (name the film). Students must develop both the visual component and the written, or *copy*, component. The images and words must convey "their experience of the film" and include "the director, the cast, the studio, excerpted critical reviews (which must be original), and a tag line," or catchy phrase that sums up the film. Finally, they must write a one-page self-analysis of their work (91–100).

Film to Lit

For many years, I asked students to translate literary texts into film scripts, but it never occurred to me to ask students to rewrite the audio-visual medium of film into a story. When I read the title of John Golden's article "Literature into Film (and Back Again): Another Look at an Old Dog," it was the words in parentheses that first grabbed my attention. In a fascinating reversal, Golden puts his theory about the power of film to inform literature into play: he shows students film clips and asks them to write diary entries for the celluloid characters they have just met. After sharing their entries in small groups, students rewrite their first-person diaries using the third-person point of view. Golden continues to build on the process of reversal by showing film clips notable for some literary aspect of their development, such as a Tim Burton's handling of setting, and students write these clips into narrative prose with an authorial focus on setting, mood, or characterization.

There's little point in writing the Shakespeare film adaptation back into a script for stage or film, but students can discover a great deal about their reading of a character, conflict, or theme by rewriting a scene from the film into narrative prose. Using Golden's process of reversal, students can write haunting descriptions of Venice using the opening scene from Orson Welles's 1952 *Othello* or Oliver Parker's 1995 *Othello*. They can write a psychological study of a troubled character or turn the controversial events of a film into the stuff of digital news.

The Producers

Having students select a scene from a play by William Shakespeare; adapt it to a film script; storyboard it; cast and rehearse it; scout locations; beg, borrow, or (well, don't steal) buy a digital camera or cell phone; and then film and produce their own scene is the most unforgettable way to learn not only about film production but also about transmediating Shakespeare's literary text to film. In the process, students learn first-hand the complexity of creative collaboration and produce more than a five-minute film clip. More often than not, they produce a memory of high school that outlives all the rest.

Years ago when I taught in a private school for boys in East Boston, I believed that the seniors in English 12 were up to the challenge of filming a scene from *Hamlet*. Seduced by the siren song of nongender casting and open campus for seniors, I enthusiastically supported their choice of scene and set—they would reenact the burial of Ophelia on the shores of Constitution Beach, and they would begin filming on location while I stayed behind to teach ninth graders. I would catch up with them during my prep period.

When I got to the beach, I found a Boston Police cruiser with flashing lights pulled onto the sidewalk, a freshly dug hole about the size of a teenage boy, and students chatting nervously with a police officer. The officer was laughing. Someone in a three-decker house across the street from the beach had called the police, convinced that a gang of murderers was burying its victim, alive. Luckily, this media-savvy group of students kept the camera rolling, and their film footage had suddenly become the raw material of a Shakespeare documentary.

All the world's a set.

8 Reading Shakespeare onto Film

What seest thou else
In the dark backward and abysm of time?
            The Tempest 1.2.61–62

Long ago, I worried about time and fell into the habit of checking the classroom clock to see how little of it we had before the bell would ring again. While researching and writing this book, I worried that there wasn't enough time even in the Shakespeare elective to learn with young adults how to read Shakespeare in triplicate, as the stuff of literature, theater, and film. Looking at studies on 21st century literacies (note the plural) and at the Common Core State Standards' distinctions between literary, informational, and media texts, I worry that we don't have time to teach it all—reading, writing, speaking, listening, viewing, producing, and publishing in multiple modes. What will we gain? What will we lose? This chapter outlines a process by which teachers can learn to trust our students more, even as we learn to trust time itself.

To save time, we have options. The good people at the Folger Shakespeare Library's Teaching Shakespeare Institute (TSI) tell us that we don't have to teach the entire play: to free up time for performance-based learning, we can focus on the most compelling scenes in a play and provide students with scene summaries to fill the gaps in plot. We can teach an abridged play: recently published, the 30-Minute Shakespeare series includes a dozen of Shakespeare's plays abridged and edited by Nick Newlin. A third time-saving option is to focus on a theme and to select scenes from Shakespeare that speak, each in its own way, to us now, four hundred years later.

In 2006, while teaching at the Folger's TSI and with the guidance of scholar Margaret Maurer, I gathered from eight of the plays a collection of scenes that focuses on the relationship between fathers and daughters. Students read the scenes and explored the characters, conflicts, and themes in brief discussions and informal performances. One of the advantages of reading Shakespeare this way is that even as students narrow their focus on a specific topic, their perspectives expand as they become acquainted with plays most will never read in high school: *King Lear, Pericles, The Taming of the Shrew, The Tempest*. When the two-week unit ended, I knew the project deserved fuller development but succumbed to the pressures of time and moved on to the next whole play. The unfinished business of the first project set the stage for the next.

In his documentary, *Looking for Richard*, Al Pacino asks, "What gets between us and Shakespeare?" Part of me wondered whether our media-saturated culture, one of the forces that draws twenty-first-century learners away from reading complex literary texts, could be enlisted to help bring students back to literature. But that wasn't all. Anyone who works in a school is constantly aware of the group dynamics, the roles, relationships, and issues of rank that somehow reconnect us on a different scale to Shakespeare's hierarchical world. *What gets between us and others?* I wondered. *What separates and divides us, and how can art, Shakespeare's art, help to make us whole?* Some of the answers, I thought, might be found in a transmediation project that invites Shakespeare's outsiders into our classrooms and our lives.

Inspired by Pacino's hybrid documentary and guided by the writing of Canadian filmmaker and educator Nikos Theodosakis and Illinois English teacher Joe Bucolo, author of the article "The Bard in the Bathroom," I constructed over time a curriculum for a unit of study that bridges gaps between old and new media and between "them" and "us." And as I enlisted colleagues in this endeavor, I learned that the focus of a Shakespeare transmediation project does not have to be a collection of themed excerpts. Colleagues at Revere High School readily adapted the material in this chapter to the required reading of an entire play, and then to the genre of novels. As a postreading student project, for example, some teachers challenged students to transmediate their reading of one scene from a Shakespeare play into a theatrical and cinematic documentary; some asked students to transmediate their reading of the first three acts of a play, or the opening chapters of a novel, into a film trailer. In each case, their day 1 begins roughly where day 6 on the project calendar ends.

One Day at a Time

The sections that follow correspond to the days in the project calendar, Handout 8.1. The days are approximations: students will be absent, equipment will fail, fire alarms will sound. But in the space of about three weeks, worry as I did about time, students wrenched from the school calendar with an unlineal hand a crown of student-centered achievement.

Day 1

To introduce students to the theme of outsiders, I ask a focus question: "What things separate and divide us and push the less powerful to the edges of our world?" Beginning with "Rules," the first responses in 2011 seemed broad and abstract, but when students named school as a force of separation and division, the question began to feel more personal (see Figure 8.1). It was time to introduce them to Shakespeare's outsiders.

It begins with Handout 8.2, the context chart. After reading aloud the names of the seven characters highlighted in the first box and explaining that the two focus questions in the last box will guide our reading of the scenes tomorrow, I ask seven students to volunteer to read aloud the contextual information for each play. Then students break into small groups and each group receives a graphic map of one of the plays; Handout 8.3 includes a collection of play maps drawn for this project by student Jennifer Sao. In groups, students attempt to read the plot from beginning to end. Because Sao's artwork is so detailed, enlarging the maps helps students do this kind of close visual reading. (Before I had this collection of graphic maps, I made word cloud graphic

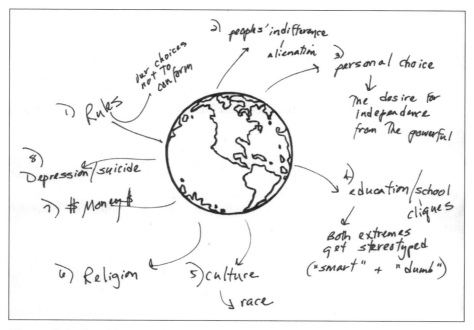

Figure 8.1. Graphic organizer that developed from our focus question.

maps by uploading the word-frequency lists of each play into a Wordle document.) After about twenty minutes, each group uses the document reader to project their map and, based on their tentative reading of the graphic map, introduce us to the characters and conflicts in the play.

Before day 1 ends, I distribute the final production project described in Handout 8.4 so that students can begin to think about separation and division not only in the context of literary conflict but also in the context of old and new literacies.

Days 2–3

The first description of students who are "college and career ready" in the 2011 Common Core State Standards (CCSS) begins with the statement, "They demonstrate independence," and argues that college and career-ready students "can, without significant scaffolding, comprehend and evaluate complex texts" (9). Shakespeare is one of the most frequently named authors of complex literary texts in the CCSS. Reading Shakespeare with less dependence on teachers and greater interdependence among themselves should be an overarching goal for students in the English language arts classroom. The raucous group reading sessions chronicled in Pacino's *Looking for Richard* provide a working model of the kind of active, collaborative, lifelong reading and risk-taking that Shakespeare's complex text requires.

Because student ownership is fundamental to effective group work, the negotiations begin here. After distributing the scripts (Handout 8.5) for the seven scenes to every student, I instruct students to form themselves into teams of five; then I ask each team to select any three of the seven scenes to read together. Borrowing from literacy coach Christina Porter's work in adapting the reciprocal teaching model to reading Shakespeare, I distribute the five reciprocal teaching role sheets to each group, and each student in each group chooses one of the five active reading roles of questioner, clarifier, summarizer, predictor, and connector (see *Reading Shakespeare with Young Adults* [Dakin], Chapter 9, Figures 9.1–9.5, for the specific handouts). Teams read three scenes, and then each team member prepares to lead the follow-up discussion based on the reading role each student plays.

Depending on the age and ability levels of students and the length of each teaching block (at my school, we currently teach in eighty-minute blocks), some groups may not be able to read three scenes and prepare their reciprocal reading roles in two days, but that's okay. Simply encourage those groups to limit their work to one or two scenes they are most interested in. When it comes to close, active reading of Shakespeare, less text almost always enables deeper, closer reading.

Through this process, teams usually arrive at their choice of the one scene they will produce together, but before they do I distribute a character chart (Handout 8.6), and from their group discussions of the outsiders in the scenes they have read, each team prepares notes and shares with the whole group their readings of Kate, Caliban, Shylock, Hermione, Othello, Edmund, and Viola. Handout 8.7 is a compendium of notes students have written about Shakespeare's outsiders.

Day 4

Guided by the glossary of film terms (Handout 3.1) and a viewing guide that focuses attention on the cinematic (Handout 5.4 or 6.1), we actively view as much of the working model as time permits in one period, looking like never before for Richard. Student Yosselin Guzman filled the white spaces of her handout (see Figure 8.2) with perceptive observations about the relationship between camera and content. She writes, for example, "When Al Pacino is talking about something that interests him and he is passionate about there are a lot of close-ups." Before day 4 ends, I distribute the project role sheet, Handout 8.8, so that students have time to consider which individual responsibilities they most want to assume.

Having students go through a job application process for the roles in each of the three stages does ensure a greater sense of student ownership of the roles, but in this and many performance and production projects the roles and stages shift; the only role that repeats itself in every stage of this project is that of director. So instead of a formal job application process, I ask students to choose the roles they will play in stage 1, knowing that readers will become actors and discussion leaders will become interviewers in stage 2, and camera operators will become editors in stage 3.

Days 5–6

Though most classrooms can be made to accommodate the stage 1 readings, filming these readings in a room where twenty or thirty students are reading, rereading, and discussing different scenes at once severely affects the audio quality at a stage when distinct human voices need to be heard in the video recording. So I reserve corners of the school learning commons for the filming of the stage 1 readings. This also helps the discussion leader research for immediate answers to questions about text and context.

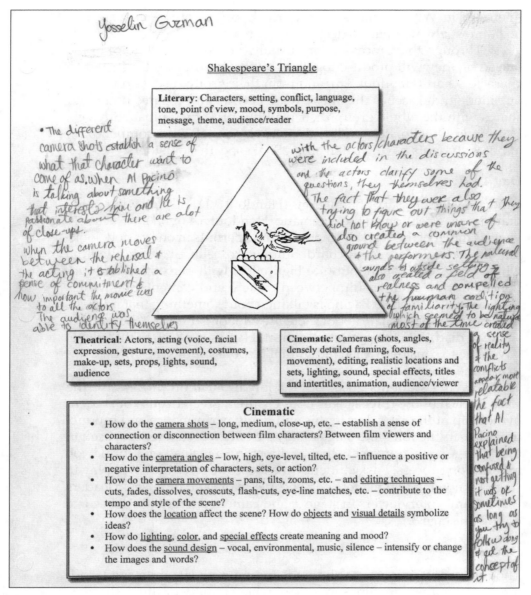

Yosselin Guzman

Shakespeare's Triangle

Literary: Characters, setting, conflict, language, tone, point of view, mood, symbols, purpose, message, theme, audience/reader

• The different camera shots establish a sense of what that character want to come of as. When Al Pacino is talking about something that interests him and he is passionate about there are alot of close-ups.

When the camera moves between the rehearsal & the acting it established a sense of commitment & how important the movie was to all the actors.

The audience was able to identify themselves

with the actors/characters because they were included in the discussions and the actors clarify some of the questions, they themselves had. The fact that they were also trying to figure out things that they did not know or were unsure of also created a common ground between the audience & the performers. The natural sounds & outside settings also created a field of realness and compelled the human condition of familiarity. The lighting which seemed to be natural most of the time created a sense of reality & the conflicts appear more relatable.

The fact that Al Pacino explained that being confused & not getting it was OK sometimes as long as you try to follow along & get the concept of it.

Theatrical: Actors, acting (voice, facial expression, gesture, movement), costumes, make-up, sets, props, lights, sound, audience

Cinematic: Cameras (shots, angles, densely detailed framing, focus, movement), editing, realistic locations and sets, lighting, sound, special effects, titles and intertitles, animation, audience/viewer

Cinematic

- How do the <u>camera shots</u> – long, medium, close-up, etc. – establish a sense of connection or disconnection between film characters? Between film viewers and characters?
- How do the <u>camera angles</u> – low, high, eye-level, tilted, etc. – influence a positive or negative interpretation of characters, sets, or action?
- How do the <u>camera movements</u> – pans, tilts, zooms, etc. – and <u>editing techniques</u> – cuts, fades, dissolves, crosscuts, flash-cuts, eye-line matches, etc. – contribute to the tempo and style of the scene?
- How does the <u>location</u> affect the scene? How do <u>objects</u> and <u>visual details</u> symbolize ideas?
- How do <u>lighting</u>, <u>color</u>, and <u>special effects</u> create meaning and mood?
- How does the <u>sound design</u> – vocal, environmental, music, silence – intensify or change the images and words?

Figure 8.2. Yosselin's marked-up version of Shakespeare's triangle.

Transmediation Project Spin-offs

At this point in the project calendar, between days 6 and 7, colleagues Althea Terenzi, Matt Despres, and Allison Casper began the work of adapting this project to their course calendars. Each teacher found a way to adapt the transmediation project to their sophomore English classes, all of which were reading or had just finished reading *Macbeth*. Terenzi crafted the first project spin-off by having her students document the process of performing and filming act 5, scene 5. Guided by the essential question, "What is the creative process for translating a text to film?," Terenzi condensed the project calendar to five days; students applied for roles to play in the production, interviewed "experts," performed the scene, filmed the entire process, and designed a rubric. Then they planned a film-fest, creating posters to hang throughout the building and inviting guests. To save production time, Terenzi edited the footage into final cuts, and on the fifth day her classroom was the site of a world premiere. She wrote questions for the performers and put them on blue index cards—"like 'Inside the Actors' Studio,' though I'm sure that detail was lost on them!"—and after each viewing, she conducted a Q&A session with the stars. "Student responses were so reflective and positive," she said. "I have never seen my students so proud of themselves and what they were able to create together."

Allison Casper was eager to build on work we had done together with the commercial triangle and Shakespeare film posters (see Chapter 2). Just as I had begun the process of having students storyboard a film trailer for *The Tempest* midway through our reading of that play earlier in the year, Casper wanted to take that activity to the next level by having her sophomores script, storyboard, film, and produce trailers for their own vision of a film adaptation of *Macbeth*. Her students brainstormed a list of abstract nouns that name the conflicts in the play and then formed small production teams and connected their choice of abstract nouns to specific events and lines in the first three acts of *Macbeth*. In a period of seven school days, Casper's students scripted, storyboarded, filmed, and edited their own thirty-second film trailers for *Macbeth*.

Days 7–10

Patience, persistence, and flexibility are required in these days. Beyond getting permissions and hall passes for the best locations inside our building for the stage 2 performances of scenes, the extent to which production equipment—cameras, mics, computers equipped with video-editing software—is available to students will impact the process. If video cameras, for example, are not available for filming stages 1 and 2, students can use cell phones and electronic pads and laptops equipped with built-in cameras, but they can expect some complications during stage 3. If the experts students choose to interview—often but not always teachers and administrators—are not available when our class meets, students may need to borrow a camera before or after school to interview them.

Some things, however, will go better than expected: Colleague and actor George Hannah selflessly offered to give up his free period on several consecutive days during stage 2 to coach students as they worked on speaking their lines with clarity and conviction. When colleague Matt Despres adapted this project to his sophomores' reading of *Macbeth*, he picked up a camera and periodically interviewed his students about the process of reading, performing, and filming Shakespeare. Knowing he could not allot three weeks to the project, Despres presented students with a six-day plan that expanded to nine. "In nearly every interview I filmed and reflection I collected, the most common response," Despres noted, "was a need for more time." Yet though his sophomores could have worked on this project for the rest of the year, he admitted, every group completed the work by the deadline and in time for the screening. "Students who had labored through the text and expressed disinterest in the project at first were staying until five and six o'clock at night, rehearsing scenes and perfecting shots," Despres acknowledged in an email. "Groups were working simultaneously in the library, chorus room, auditorium, television studio and even a bathroom (!) with absolute professionalism, drive and creativity."

Although it may seem like an easy step to skip, constructing a storyboard of a speech or scene in Shakespeare or a script of their own requires students, at the very least, to organize material into a coherent shot sequence with a beginning, middle, and end. As a pre*filming* tool, storyboarding helps students to pursue the visual and auditory possibilities of a story they will tell not only with words but also with camera shots and angles, lighting, editing, and sound. As a pre*production* tool, storyboards challenge students to work constructively with the video and audio clips that they have, since nothing ever goes completely according to plan and the unexpected can spark new directions and ideas. Instead of allowing students to waste precious time filming dozens of shots they either won't need or will need to reshoot, require novice directors, camera operators, and reader-actors to discuss and storyboard the ways in which they can use the tools of cinematography to transmediate Shakespeare's words into Almereyda's "parallel visual language" as a necessary prerequisite to filming.

Storyboard templates are readily available online, but I have modified the storyboard templates of film-in-the-classroom authors such as John Golden and Nikos Theodosakis into a collection that I use interchangeably, depending on the complexity of the project and the needs of students. Some modification of Figure 2.5 is the simplest in that it relies mainly on student sketches of each frame and requires little in the way of overt technical notations. Handout 7.2 is an example of an intermediate template that relies on a series of shot sketches and some combination of notes on camera work, action, and sound. Handout 8.9, distributed in multiple copies to accommodate the approximate number of shots needed for a scene performance or a final production, requires students to address the artistic and technical specifics of a shot sequence. In addition to these templates, students can construct a "tellingboard" by simply sketching stick figures and words onto sticky notes and applying and rearranging them on pieces of plain paper (Rief 202).

Though I had worried at the beginning of the course about devoting so much class time to a project that wanders far from the printed word, I learned that the act of reading Shakespeare remains essential in this production project even as the project keeps building in complexity and intensity—from reading to speaking and planning and moving, questioning and interviewing, storyboarding, filming, editing, producing, and problem-solving. The problems will not all be academic or technical; some students will work together more cooperatively than others. I felt the tension among students that comes from deadlines, differences of opinion, and real or perceived disrespect. An audio–video production project is a conundrum of careful planning and chaos; it is messy and meaningful, like life.

Day 11

At computers equipped with programs for audio and video production, stage 3 begins when students gather in companies to view as much of their raw footage as possible, indicating to their director and editor the scenes and minutes they consider essential to their company's documentary. In addition to the prefilming storyboard, teams begin to construct a preproduction storyboard that chronicles their journey around Shakespeare's triangle.

Days 12–14

After they have listened to their group's ideas about the selection and sequence of shots and storyboarded the shots they consider most necessary to the documentary, the director and editor begin work on the rough cut. A *rough cut* is a first draft shot sequence cut together in the right order but without the addition of appropriate visual transitions, title shots, or music.

While directors and editors assemble rough cuts, I take advantage of the downtime to engage the remaining students in the task of establishing assessment criteria. It always helps to begin with tangible models. Before I had a collection of student productions from the previous year, I asked students to nominate in Academy Award style their own Best Picture films, movies they had seen recently or in the past, and then choose one and write a brief film review that describes the most effective literary, theatrical, and cinematic elements of that film. Though the formal elements of writing a film review are not part of this project, two excellent guides for writing film reviews can be found in Appendix 2 of William Costanzo's *Great Films and How to Teach Them* and Chapter 2 of *Reel Conversations* by Alan B. Teasley and Ann Wilder. After students write, I hand out multicolored highlighters and ask students to color-code the words and phrases they used to praise a film: one color for words that praise the story, another for acting, a third for sound, and a fourth for the camera work and editing techniques. Finally, we read Emily C. Bartels's 1997 film review of *Looking for Richard*, annotate it for a critic's criteria and commentary, and add to our lists. From these activities, students generate the criteria for assessing the work of their own film production.

But in 2012, I had a collection of six Shakespeare documentaries produced by students in 2011, so while the directors and editors were working on rough cuts, the other members of their teams viewed this collection of "anchor papers"; among the projects were exemplary models of reading, performing, filming, and editing. We stopped after each documentary to talk about what the students did well last year and what they could have done better; at the end of the viewings, students awarded "stars" in the style of the five-star rating system to the work of their peers, most of whom had graduated in 2011. Somewhere between the rough cut and the final cut, team members talked again with their directors and editors about what they had learned from these models.

From these raw materials, students working in small groups use the rubric template in Handout 8.10 to organize and articulate their understanding of what students should know and be able to do when transmediating Shakespeare. In 2012 the students in the Shakespeare elective determined that they should be able to read literature closely; perform a scene; and use video, audio, and editing tools to relate the complex process of learning as a story. Handout 8.11, the project rubric, combines their best ideas, but each year I will continue the process of including students in the assessment of their own work, generating the criteria and objectives of success.

Meanwhile, at the computers student editors and directors assemble the rough cut into a final cut, trimming shots and scenes down like wordy sentences to their sparest and most essential length. One of the common shortcomings of student video productions is the excessive amount of time a single shot or scene runs, which is paradoxical considering the flash-cut editing that drives popular culture. For this project, I urge editors to produce a final cut that doesn't exceed ten minutes. Though the actual process may not move forward in a purely linear fashion, editors and producers work on the title cuts, adding appropriate visual transitions in addition to the common cut between shots (fades, dissolves, sweeps, etc.) and then music, sound effects, and voice-over narration. The final video is readied for export and viewing.

Day 15

Located in the darkness of our school's television studio, the film festival generates the kind of nervous energy that most students experience only vicariously through news entertainment footage of celebrity events. After the final viewing, to help me learn how to do this better next time, students rearrange themselves like puzzle pieces into new group configurations to create a do's and don'ts list (see Figure 8.3).

If, under the constraints of time and the school calendar, this project were to conclude well before day 15, and if students' critical thinking were assessed using an objective multiple-choice test on Shakespeare's three faces or a five-paragraph essay in response to this project's essential question—*How should we read Shakespeare in the twenty-first century?*—neither students nor their teachers would know the extent to which experiential learning, collaboration, and guided risk-taking support students' understanding of complex texts and problems, ownership of the learning goals, and positive self-identification (Kelly 21–23). Instead we have a collection of student-produced documentaries that asks and authentically answers essential questions

Do ...	Don't ...
➤ Begin and end with Shakespeare's words ➤ Really get into the scene ➤ Schedule interviews in advance ➤ Learn about context and history: step outside of the scene ➤ Work with people you respect: respect people you work with ➤ Plan everything and be prepared for things to go wrong ➤ Be creative, patient, organized, committed ➤ Film everything ➤ Have fun	➤ Read Shakespeare like blah-blah-blah ➤ Overthink the words: feel them too ➤ Waste time ➤ Be afraid to speak your mind but don't exclude or boss others ➤ Underestimate a team member ➤ Be someone else in front of a camera; be yourself ➤ Over-organize: good things accidentally happen ➤ Be afraid ➤ Text while driving or you will die and not be able to read Shakespeare!

Figure 8.3. Do's and don'ts of the final production project.

about Shakespeare and the human experience onscreen and in voice-over, with camera shots that thoughtfully frame faces located in place and time, shot sequences that achieve a narrative purpose, title shots that punctuate, and music that reinforces mood. Some of the student production projects cited in this chapter can be viewed at my website, www.readingshakespeare.org.

In the time we have, there is no way to do it all, but students teach us that somehow we can. To understand what we learn when we explore the space between us and Shakespeare, I constructed a final reflection (Handout 8.12) inspired by the revised Bloom's taxonomy (Anderson and Krathwohl) and an article written by Peter Pappas, "The Reflective Student." This chapter and this book about transmediating Shakespeare end not in a teacher's voice, but in the voice of students who will take Shakespeare's rough magic with them into the twenty-first century. Gentle breath of theirs our sails must fill, or else our project fails.

> I have discovered that those who read and perform Shakespeare need to get inside themselves first.
>
> —Javier Muñoz

> I learned that everyone is an outsider and that is why Shakespeare's plays revolve around them and us.
>
> —Edward Adams

> Communicating, working together, and discovering our inner Shakespeare—I've never done as much thinking as I did in this class with Shakespeare.
>
> —Sophia DesJardins

My favorite part about the whole project was trying to fit into a character that I didn't think was me.

—Jonathan Esmurria

I was camera woman and editor, and this project helped me put my thoughts in order in a way that makes sense to anyone.

—Kelly Avalos

It seems as if Shakespeare himself understood well what it is like to be an outsider. In almost all of his plays, there seems to be an outsider with tremendous desire to be heard and understood.

—Xuyen Mai

I learned that reading Shakespeare is a lot harder than performing it, that any good performance comes from reading it first, word by word, and realizing that there are endless possibilities of meaning.

—Jenelle Worcester

I learned something about reading and performing Shakespeare, that the words matter but so do the movements and the way the words are spoken. This frustrated me, because I wanted a better sound.

—Jordan Rodriguez

Shakespeare is on par with Einstein, but somehow it was fun reading and acting out characters without making a fool of myself. Okay, actually I did make a fool of myself but it's fine since Shakespeare classes are about fun, not perfection.

—Charlie Wongwajarachot

Being behind the camera made me understand how important the angles are, the ways in which we see or don't see others.

—Rachel Murray

Time management is crucial. If you spend either too much or too little time on a certain thing, the whole project can be affected.

—Estrella Vargas

One thing I learned about communicating with film is that you need to communicate from the camera to the audience.

—Aaron Leon

I learned that final production allowed us to amplify the message. Editing film required us to think in many dimensions.

—Marissa Maccioli

Working in teams can be tough, but it taught me the importance of cooperation. It was hard to act out the scene and write a storyboard and then leave the editing and final production to someone else. I can imagine Shakespeare feeling the same way when he gave his plays to the actors. They could do whatever they wanted with his work, and he had to trust that they would interpret the spirit of his words.

—Lindsay Chorlian

Working in teams somehow makes things one-of-a-kind.

—Jeffrey Chhay

Leadership is a very important skill to have when working in groups, but humility is even more important.

—Taylor Oliva

I learned that Shakespeare's outsiders are actually mirror images of us.

—Diego Mancia

I had the privilege to learn Shakespeare in the most amazing way possible. We not only read the great works of a man who many dismiss as "too complicated" and "outdated," we learned to appreciate Shakespeare as literature and as play.

—Yosselin Guzman

We are very much alone. Regardless of how close we feel to those around us, we live locked within our own skulls, unable to fully fathom the thoughts or intentions of others. Shakespeare's characters—Hamlet, Othello, Hermione, Katharina, Shylock, Viola, and more—face similar struggles, which raises the question: Are many facing the same lonely struggle together, alone? Shakespeare requires us to give ourselves to the nouns, verbs, adjectives, and sounds until we fall into that character. Is this why Shakespeare's art matters?

—Lillian McKinley

This project and this course and this writer remind us that we are not alone.

—Juliana Panzini

Shakespeare gives voice to what we try to hide inside.

—Jennifer Sao

What I truly learned is that we are not professionals or scholars and we cannot let that discourage us. We did not understand that at first, but I can say now that I helped to bring Shakespeare back to life.

—Kate Ferrante

Appendix: Handouts

Handout 1.1.
Introduction to the Principles of Visual Composition
Question Sets

Display a poster of a Shakespeare film and lead a whole-group discussion:

First Question Set (Framing *the subject***)**
- Who or what is framed inside the borders of this image?
- Inside the outer frame, do you see smaller frames—geometric shapes such as circles, squares, or lines—that draw your attention?

Second Question Set (Placement *of the subject in relation to the camera***)**
- Who, or what, is the subject of this image?
- What is the distance between the camera and the subject—a close-up shot? A medium shot? A long shot? How does camera distance influence the way you see the subject?
- What is the angle of the camera? Higher than the subject? Lower? Eye level? How does the camera angle influence the way you see the subject?

Third Question Set (Subject Arrangement)
- Who or what is in the foreground?
- Is there a middle ground in this image? Who or what is in the middle ground?
- Who or what is farthest from view?
- What does the subject arrangement imply about the relationships in this image?

Fourth Question Set (Lighting and **Color)**
- Where is the light in this image most intense? Who or what is being highlighted?
- What color is most intense in this image?
- What is the effect of darkness or shadows?
- How would you describe the mood of the image, based on its light and color?

Handout 1.2. Constructing the Filmic Image

Imagine the five principles of visual composition—*framing, placement, subject arrangement, lighting,* and *color*—as five different jobs at a construction site.

Framing = The Carpenter

Framing refers to both the outer borders of a shot or image and the inner frames within the frame such as windows, doorways, arches, or any geometric pattern that focuses attention on a particular space, object, or person.

Questions	Notes
▪ Who or what is framed inside the borders of this image? ▪ Inside the outer frame, do you see smaller frames—geometric shapes such as circles, squares, or lines? On what do they focus your attention?	

Placement = The Surveyor

Placement refers to the relationship between the camera and the subject. This can mean the distance of the camera—long shot, medium shot, close-up—and the angle of the camera, as well as the effect these things have on the viewer's perception of the subject.

Questions	Notes
▪ Who, or what, is the subject of this image? ▪ What is the distance between the camera and the subject—a close-up shot? A medium shot? A long shot? How does camera distance influence the way you see the subject? ▪ What is the angle of the camera? High? Low? Eye level? How does the camera angle influence the way you see the subject?	

continued on next page

Handout 1.2

Subject arrangement = The Interior Designer

Subject arrangement is the physical arrangement of people, objects, and background in the frame; these can convey or imply relationships. Arrangement can be, and often is, layered, with some things in the foreground, some in the middle ground, and some in the background.

Questions	Notes
▪ Who or what is in the foreground? ▪ Is there a middle ground in this image? Who or what is in the middle ground? ▪ Who or what is farthest from view? ▪ What does the subject arrangement imply about the relationships in this image?	

Lighting = The Electrician   Color = The Painter

Lighting is the intensity of light, or the lack of light, or the contrast between light and shadow in a frame. **Color** is the palette of hues in the image, and as with lighting, its effect can be manipulated through intensity and contrast.

Questions	Notes
▪ Where is the light in this image most intense? Who or what is being highlighted? ▪ What color is most intense in this image? ▪ What is the effect of darkness or shadows? ▪ How would you describe the mood of the image, based on its light and color?	

Reading Shakespeare Film First by Mary Ellen Dakin © 2012 NCTE.

Handout 2.1. Focused Viewing: The Elements of a Film Trailer

Film trailers can be divided into a **beginning, middle**, and **end** using this formula:

> **Act 1** of the trailer establishes the major conflicts of the film.
> **Act 2** of the trailer drives the conflicts toward a climax.
> **Act 3** of the trailer concludes with emotionally charged signature music (this might be popular music familiar to the audience or a symphonic composition) and a dramatic visual montage.

First Viewings

Chunk the film trailer into a beginning, middle, and end, using these markers as a guide:

Act 1: The Conflict
What major conflicts in Shakespeare's play are established in the trailer? How are the conflicts established using images, sounds, and dialogue? What characters and relationships are introduced?

Act 2: The Climax
What event or visual image in the trailer marks a major confrontation or turning point in the conflict?

Act 3: The Conclusion
What does the final sequence of shots suggest about the film? How do music and sound contribute to the dramatic effect of the closing?

Final Viewings

Words, words words . . .
- Is there a voice-over narrator? What does the voice-over narrator contribute to the audience's comprehension of the trailer?
- What words from Shakespeare's play are spoken in the trailer? Why these words (from the average number of 22,595 words per play)?
- What print words appear in some frames of the trailer? Are they words from Shakespeare's play? What is their purpose—to explain, to narrate, to persuade?

Sounds and sweet airs . . .
- How is sound (vocal, environmental, sound effects, music, silence) used in the film trailer?
- What tone does the sound track convey?

Dramatis personae . . .
- What does the cast run contribute to the final appeal of the film trailer?
- What might the final credits—the producer, director, studio, production company, distributor, etc.—add to the audience's understanding of the film?

O brave new world . . .
- Is Shakespeare's play modified or changed to appeal to a modern audience? What are the effects of these changes?
- How is Shakespeare reshaped by popular culture?

PRODUCT / PRODUCER / CONSUMER

Reading Shakespeare Film First by Mary Ellen Dakin © 2012 NCTE.

Handout 3.1. Glossary of Film Terms

Excerpted and adapted from *Reading in the Dark*, John Golden; *Reel Conversations*, Alan B. Teasley and Ann Wilder; *Looking at Movies*, Richard Barsam and Dave Monahan; *Shakespeare and Film*, Samuel Crowl; *Great Films and How to Teach Them*, William V. Costanzo; *Anatomy of Film*, Bernard F. Dick; *Shakespeare on Film*, Carolyn Jess-Cooke

FRAMING / CAMERA SHOTS

Framing refers to the content of the shot—who or what is in the shot.

Long shot (LS): A shot taken from some distance; shows the full subject and perhaps the surrounding scene as well. An **aerial shot** is filmed from a crane or an aircraft.

Extreme long shot (ELS): Taken from a great distance with a wide view. The subject may be too small to be recognized. An ELS is called an **establishing shot** when it defines the location.

Medium shot (MS): In-between LS and CS; people are seen from the waist up.

Close-up: A single image takes up most of the screen; for example, an actor's face.

Extreme close-up: A very close shot of a small detail that fills a screen; for example, an eye.

CAMERA ANGLES

Low angle: Camera is below the subject; usually has the effect of making the subject look larger than normal.

High angle: Camera is above the subject; usually has the effect of making the subject look smaller than normal.

Eye level: Accounts for 90 to 95 percent of the shots seen because it is most natural; camera is even with the key character's eyes.

Overhead: The camera looks down on the subject from a fixed location directly above.

Dutch angle: The camera is tilted sideways on the horizontal line (also called **canted angle**); used to add tension to a frame; usually has the effect of distorting the subject.

Wide angle: Shoots a wide area and makes the subject seem farther away.

CAMERA MOVEMENT

Pan: The horizontal movement left or right of a stationary camera mounted on a tripod.

Tilt: The vertical movement up or down of a stationary camera mounted on a tripod.

Dolly: The camera is moving with the action—on a track, on wheels, or held by hand.

Zoom: The camera is stationary but the lens shifts, making the image appear to grow larger or smaller. A **slam zoom** is shot at high speed.

Handheld: Small portable cameras that produce the shaky images associated with news footage.

Steadicam: A device that allows a portable camera to closely and rapidly follow, or lead, the action without shakiness.

FOCUS

Deep focus: When the foreground and background are equally in focus.

Soft focus: When a director intentionally puts the subject of a shot slightly out of focus to make the subject look softer or unclear.

Rack focus: When a director shifts the focus from one subject to another in the same shot to direct the audience's attention.

continued on next page

Handout 3.1

EDITING TECHNIQUES

The most common is a **cut** to another image. Others are:

Fade: Scene fades to black or white; often implies that time has passed.

Dissolve: An image fades into another; can create a connection between images.

Wipe: A line moves across the screen, literally wiping out one shot and replacing it with another.

Crosscut: Cutting to different action that is happening simultaneously; also called **parallel** editing.

Flashback: Movement into action that has happened previously, often signified by a change in music, voice-over narration, or a dissolve; a **flash-forward** leads us ahead in time.

Flash cut: An extremely rapid succession of different but related shots in a sequence.

Eye-line match: A shot of a person looking, then a cut to what the person sees, then a cut back for a reaction.

Montage: a dramatic sequence of rapid shots that condense events into a single narrative composition.

LIGHTING

Low-key: Scene is flooded with shadows and darkness; creates suspense/suspicion.

High-key: Scene is flooded with light; creates a bright and open-looking scene.

Neutral: Neither bright nor dark—even lighting throughout the shot.

Side lighting: Lighting from either side of a subject, leaving it half in light and half in shadow; can convey internal division, split personality, or moral ambiguity.

Bottom lighting: Direct lighting from below; can convey danger or evil.

Front/rear: Soft, direct lighting on face or back of subject; can create a halo effect that suggests innocence or goodness.

SOUND

Diegetic sound originates from something within the world of the film and characters can conceivably hear it; **nondiegetic** sound originates from outside the world of the film (an orchestral sound track or a voice-over narrator, for example).

Vocal: Dialogue (ordinary speech or theatrical), on-screen narration, and on- or off-screen voices (vocal sound produced by a large group of people). A **voice-over** is off-camera narration by a character who is not in the scene, a narrator who is not a character, or a commentator.

Environmental: Background sounds and noise that are natural to the setting and the action, though they may be produced artificially as **sound effects** to intensify the impact.

Music: Can be any combination of classical or modern and played by characters and objects in the film or by off-screen musicians, bands, and orchestras. Music contributes to the tone, mood, and themes of a film and can contribute to characterization.

Silence: The absence of sound, which can have an unsettling effect on the audience. Silence in a film reinforces the importance of images.

Reading Shakespeare Film First by Mary Ellen Dakin © 2012 NCTE.

Handout 3.2. The Three Faces of Shakespeare on Film

Literary

Who are the <u>characters</u> in the film?

What is the film's <u>setting</u>?

What happens? Briefly summarize the <u>conflict</u>.

How significant is the <u>language</u>?

What is the vocal <u>tone</u> of the dialogue?

From whose <u>point of view</u> is the story told?

Who is the film's <u>intended audience</u>?

What is the <u>mood</u> of the film?

What objects function as <u>symbols</u> in the film?

What is the film's <u>purpose</u>, beyond entertainment?

What issues and ideas seem important? What are the <u>themes</u> of the film?

Theatrical

How do the <u>actors</u> interpret the characters they play?

How do the <u>costumes</u> and <u>makeup</u> reinforce the acting?

Describe the <u>sets</u> and the most interesting <u>props</u>.

Do <u>lighting</u> and <u>color</u> contribute to the drama? How?

Does <u>sound</u> and/or <u>silence</u> contribute to the drama? How?

Cinematic

How is the scene organized into a <u>shot sequence</u>? Are the shots in the sequence related in a cause-effect pattern to help us understand what is happening, or do some shots seem unrelated, confusing, or discontinuous?

Describe the most memorable <u>photography</u>. Are there unexpected camera **shots**, camera **angles**, camera **movements**, or lens **focus**?

What <u>editing</u> techniques besides the common cut are particularly memorable?

How does the <u>sound</u> (vocal, environmental, music, silence) express and intensify the scene?

How do <u>lighting</u> and <u>color</u> create meaning and mood?

Handout 3.3. Designing Before-and-After Costumes

COSTUME DESIGNERS Needed!

Your job is to make visible Shakespeare's richly imaginative characters in King Lear.

Design before-and-after costumes and make-up for these characters that take them from the beginning of act 1 to the middle of act 2:

> King Lear
> Kent
> Edgar
> Goneril and/or Regan

Sketch your designs. Also include brief written explanations of your design choices, including such details as color, texture, and line.

Consider the historical time and geographical place. You have freedom to imagine an appropriate setting, from the ancient world to the modern; the historical sources of this play extend back in time to Britain's pre-Roman and pre-Christian past.

Consider your character's status and wealth.

Consider the symbolism of colors:

> Red, gold, purple, silver: royalty, wealth, power
> Blue: loyalty or serenity
> Green: youth, hope, but also jealousy
> Brown, grey: earth tones associated with the working and laboring classes; humility
> Black: can be associated with power and influence, and with religion, but also with mourning and mystery
> White: purity; death

Above all, your designs should capture the character's traits and the changes in status each character undergoes in acts 1 and 2.

Reading Shakespeare Film First by Mary Ellen Dakin © 2012 NCTE.

Handout 3.4. Daily Practice

DATE:

TOPIC: Reading *Romeo and Juliet* on Film

Directions: Use the Glossary of Film Terms to identify and discuss the <u>camera shot</u>, <u>camera angle</u>, and <u>lighting</u> in each frame of film:

Shot:

Angle:

Color, Lighting:

Effect:

Shot:

Angle:

Color, Lighting:

Effect:

Reading Shakespeare Film First by Mary Ellen Dakin © 2012 NCTE.

Handout 3.5. Film Terms to Know

Film Terms to Know, Part 1

Name four different **camera shots**:

1. _____   3. _____

2. _____   4. _____

Name three different ways to **focus** a camera lens:

5. _____

6. _____

7. _____

Name four different **camera angles**:

8. _____   10. _____

9. _____   11. _____

Name four different **camera movements**:

12. _____   14. _____

13. _____   15. _____

Film Terms to Know, Part 2

CAMERA SHOTS
  A. Long Shot   D. Close-up
  B. Establishing Shot   E. Extreme Close-up
  C. Medium Shot

_____ 1. Taken from a great distance with a wide view. The subject may be too small to be recognized.
_____ 2. A very close shot of a small detail that fills the screen.
_____ 3. A shot taken from some distance; shows the full subject and perhaps the surrounding scene.
_____ 4. A single image takes up most of the screen; for example, an actor's face.

continued on next page

Handout 3.5

CAMERA ANGLES

_____ 5. Camera is above the subject; makes the subject look smaller.

_____ 6. The camera looks down on the subject from a fixed location directly above.

_____ 7. Shoots a broad area and makes objects seem farther away.

_____ 8. The camera is tilted or canted to distort the subject.

Film Terms to Know, Part 3

LIGHTING

A. Low-key
B. High-key
C. Neutral

D. Bottom/side
E. Front/rear

_____ 1. Scene is flooded with light; creates bright and open-looking scene.

_____ 2. Soft, direct lighting on face or back of subject—may suggest innocence; creates a halo effect.

_____ 3. Scene is flooded with shadows and darkness; creates suspense/ suspicion.

_____ 4. Direct lighting from below or from one side; often dangerous or evil-looking, may convey split personality or moral ambiguity.

CAMERA MOVEMENT

A. Pan
B. Tilt

C. Zoom
D. Dolly

_____ 5. The camera itself is moving with the action—on a track, on wheels, or held by hand.

_____ 6. Stationary camera moves left or right.

_____ 7. Stationary camera moves up or down.

EDITING TECHNIQUES

A. Fade
B. Dissolve

C. Crosscut
D. Eye-line match

_____ 8. Cut to action that is happening simultaneously.

_____ 9. An image fades into another; can create a connection between images.

_____ 10. Scene fades to black or white; often implies time has passed.

Reading Shakespeare Film First by Mary Ellen Dakin © 2012 NCTE.

Handout 3.6. Shakespeare's Triangle: Emphasis on Theater

Literary: Characters, setting, conflict, language, tone, point of view, mood, symbols, purpose, message, theme, audience/reader

Theatrical: Actors, acting, (voice, facial expression, gesture, movement), costumes, makeup, sets, props, lights, sound, audience

Cinematic: Cameras editing, realistic locations and sets, lighting, sound, special effects, titles, and intertitles, animation, audience/viewer

Theatrical

- How do the <u>actors</u> interpret the characters they play? What character traits do they emphasize? What <u>acting</u> techniques contribute to the performance?

- How do the <u>costumes</u> and <u>makeup</u> reinforce the acting?

- Describe the main <u>set</u> and the most important <u>props</u>.

- Do <u>lighting</u> and <u>color</u> contribute to the drama? How?

- Do <u>sound</u> and/or <u>silence</u> contribute to the drama? How?

Reading Shakespeare Film First by Mary Ellen Dakin © 2012 NCTE.

Handout 4.1. From Script to Screen

Transmediating Bottom's Dream

Your task is to adapt Bottom's speech in 4.1.210–29 of *A Midsummer Night's Dream* to film by composing a screenplay. Your film will be an adaptation, spoken in Shakespeare's language.

Compose **directorial commentary** that narrates and explains your answers to these questions about the theatrical elements. Directorial commentary is written in italics and enclosed in parentheses. It is highly descriptive.

> How will you direct an **actor** to interpret Bottom? What character traits will you emphasize? What **acting** techniques—voice, facial expression, gesture, movement—will contribute to your interpretation of Bottom?

> How will the **costumes** and **makeup** reinforce the acting?

> Describe the **set** at the beginning of your commentary. Indicate what **props**, if any, your production will need.

> How will you use **lighting** and **color** to contribute to the scene?

> What **non-vocal sounds**—environmental, musical, silent—will contribute to the scene?

Compose **slug lines** for your screenplay. The slug line should be formatted in caps and should convey three points of information in this order:

EXTERIOR or INTERIOR shot / LOCATION / DAY or NIGHT
Example: EXTERIOR / ATHENIAN WOODS / DAWN

Write a new slug line when one of the three pieces of information changes.

Sample Screenplay
A Midsummer Night's Dream, Act 1, Scene 2

EXTERIOR / QUINCE'S COTTAGE / NIGHT
(A pastoral countryside, very green and lush, at sundown. A simple melody can be heard from a flute. Butterflies, tiny songbirds, and fireflies make magical swirls in the sky overhead. From four different directions along winding paths enter

continued on next page

Handout 4.1

*FLUTE, STARVELING, SNOUT, and SNUG, looking like they have just fin-
ished a day's work. They each wear simple country clothing and carry the tools of
their trades on their backs. FLUTE is playing a flute as he walks; STARVELING,
too thin for his clothing, is hungrily eating a sandwich as he walks; SNOUT
blows his nose noisily on a well-used cloth, then neatly folds it back into his
pocket; SNUG, clearly the largest man for miles around, carries a stuffed toy
beneath his arm, something his mother probably made for him long ago.*

*They approach a little English-looking cottage, home of PETER QUINCE, who
is waiting for them eagerly with a stack of "scrips" in one hand and a pencil in
the other. QUINCE is older than the others, and though a carpenter by trade,
he dresses for success in a buttoned jacket and a hat.*

*Finally, NICK BOTTOM enters, bounding down the lane with great fuss and
fanfare, waving to his "fans" as he approaches the cottage, confident of the fact
that he will be, must be, the star in this Guild production. A weaver by trade,
he has draped himself in a colorful cloak, and it swishes dramatically as he arrives at QUINCE'S cottage gate. Though the gate has been left open by SNUG,
BOTTOM closes it, then leaps over it, to punctuate his dramatic entrance.)*

QUINCE (*Excited, glad to see that all have shown up for this first rehearsal*)
Is all our company here? (*He takes a checklist/scroll from his pocket and begins
to use his pencil*)

BOTTOM (*In a booming voice, with confidence*)
You were best to call them generally, man by man, according to the scrip.

QUINCE (*With great pride, letting the scroll unroll in his hand*)
Here is the scroll of every man's name which is thought fit, through all
Athens, to play in our interlude before the Duke and the Duchess on his
wedding day . . . (*adds as an afterthought*) at night.

BOTTOM (*A bit impatient, as though Quince is doing things all wrong*)
First, good Peter Quince, say what the play treats on, then read the names
of the actors, and so grow to a point.

QUINCE (*He bows to BOTTOM'S apparent expertise, then reads in an "of-
ficial" voice*)
Marry, our play is "The most lamentable comedy and most cruel death
of Pyramus and Thisbe.". . .

Reading Shakespeare Film First by Mary Ellen Dakin © 2012 NCTE.

Handout 4.2. Comparative Viewing

Literary	Theatrical Actors and acting, costumes and makeup, set and props, lighting and color, sound	Cinematic
Characters, setting, conflict, language, tone, POV, mood, symbols, purpose, message, themes	**Clip**: *A Midsummer Night's Dream.* Directed by Max Reinhardt and William Dieterle. 1935.	Camera shots, angle, and movement; editing, location, lighting, sound, special effects, titles, animation
	In this film clip, the actor James Cagney and the directors interpret Bottom as: Theatrical evidence:	

Literary	Theatrical Actors and acting, costumes and makeup, set and props, lighting and color, sound	Cinematic
Characters, setting, conflict, language, tone, POV, mood, symbols, purpose, message, themes	**Clip**: *A Midsummer Night's Dream.* Directed by Michael Hoffman. 1999.	Camera shots, angle, and movement; editing, location, lighting, sound, special effects, titles, animation
	In this film clip, the actor Kevin Kline and the director interpret Bottom as: Theatrical evidence:	

Reading Shakespeare Film First by Mary Ellen Dakin © 2012 NCTE.

Handout 4.3. Comparative Focused Viewing: Set, Props, Costumes, Sound

Where are we? What is the mood? What do the set, props, costumes, and sound track of each film clip contribute to our first impressions of the characters, conflicts, and themes in act 1 of *Othello*? What stands out in each production?

Othello, **directed by Oliver Parker. 1995**
Your focus (check 1):
      ☐ Set and Props   ☐ Costumes   ☐ Sound

Your notes:

Othello, **directed by Trevor Nunn. 1990**
Your focus (check 1):
      ☐ Set and Props   ☐ Costumes   ☐ Sound

Your notes:

Othello, **directed by Orson Welles. 1952**
Your focus (check 1):
      ☐ Set and Props   ☐ Costumes   ☐ Sound

Your notes:

O, **directed by Tim Blake Nelson. 2001**
Your focus (check 1):
      ☐ Set and Props   ☐ Costumes   ☐ Sound

Your notes:

Reading Shakespeare Film First by Mary Ellen Dakin © 2012 NCTE.

Handout 4.4. Comparative Focused Viewing: Comedy

Watch several film performances of *A Midsummer Night's Dream* act 5, the play-within-a-play, focusing on the theatrical elements of comedy. Note the theatrical details in each production that contribute to Shakespeare's comic dialogue.

MND, directed by Max Reinhardt and William Dieterle.
1935

What's funny? **Your focus** (check one):
☐ Acting   ☐ Costumes & Makeup   ☐ Sets & Props

☐ Lighting & Color   ☐ Sound (vocal, environmental, music, silence)

Your notes:

MND, directed by Michael Hoffman. 1999

What's funny? **Your focus** (check one):
☐ Acting   ☐ Costumes & Makeup   ☐ Sets & Props

☐ Lighting & Color   ☐ Sound (vocal, environmental, music, silence)

Your notes:

Handout 5.1. Seeing the Unexpected

shot: one continuous, uninterrupted run of the camera

shot sequence: a series of shots edited together to achieve a unified narrative purpose

The Expected

We can expect a shot sequence to begin with an **establishing shot** that locates the action, establishes the mood, and begins a **sequence** of related shots, **long shots** for actions and **closer shots** for reactions; we expect shots to be combined by means of invisible **cuts** in a continuous, **cause-effect pattern**; we expect the **tempo** of each shot to vary but the timing of shots to feel natural and not too rapid or too slow; we expect the **final shot** in the sequence to dissolve/fade.

Shot sequence title:_____ Number of shots:_____

- Is the first shot an **establishing shot**?

- Do the **long shots** tend to show action? Do the **closer shots** tend to show reaction?

- Are all the shots related in a **cause-effect pattern**, or do some shots seem disconnected from the scene?

- Is the **tempo** of some shots very rapid? Does the camera linger too slowly in some shots?

- Does the **final shot** bring closure to the scene in any way other than a fade to black?

The Unexpected
How does the unexpected intensify your response to this production and this shot sequence?

Handout 5.2. Hamlet in Voice-Over:
Five Speeches, Summarized and Annotated

	SPEECH 1: 1.2.141–64	

While Denmark celebrates the marriage of Hamlet's mother to Hamlet's uncle, Hamlet remembers his dead father's devotion to his mother and expresses shock at her hasty remarriage to his father's brother.	That it should come to this:
	 But two months dead—nay, not so much, not two.
	
	 So excellent a king, that was to this
	 Hyperion to a satyr; so loving to my mother
	 That he might not beteem the winds of heaven
	 Visit her face too roughly. Heaven and earth,
	 Must I remember? Why, she would hang on him
	 As if increase of appetite had grown
	 By what it fed on.
	
	     And yet, within a month
	 (Let me not think on 't; frailty, thy name is woman!),
	 A little month, or ere those shoes were old
	 With which she followed my poor father's body,
	 Like Niobe, all tears—why she, even she
	 (O, God, a beast that wants discourse of reason
	 Would have mourn'd longer!), married with my uncle,
	 My father's brother, but no more like my father
	 Than I to Hercules. Within a month,
	 Ere yet the salt of most unrighteous tears
	 Had left the flushing in her gallèd eyes,
	 She married.
	
	     O, most wicked speed, to post
	 With such dexterity to incestuous sheets!
	 It is not, nor it cannot come to good.
	 But break, my heart, for I must hold my tongue.
		Hyperion: a sun god
		 satyr: a mythological creature, part human and part goat
		
		 frailty: weakness
		 Niobe: a grief-stricken mother in mythology
		 wants: lacks
		
		 Hercules: a hero of great strength in mythology
		
		 post: hurry, race
		 incestuous: intercourse between close kin

Hamlet acknowledges conflicting religious beliefs about the marriage of in-laws as incest.		

continued on next page

Handout 5.2

	SPEECH 2: 1.4.43–62	

While King Claudius and Queen Gertrude celebrate their marriage late into the night, Hamlet stands guard with friend Horatio and soldier Marcellus.
 	
The Ghost appears to them and Hamlet tries to make it speak.
	Angels and ministers of grace, defend us!
	Be thou a spirit of health or goblin damned,
	Bring with thee airs from heaven or blasts from hell,
	Be thy intents wicked or charitable,
	Thou com'st in such a questionable shape
	That I will speak to thee. I'll call thee "Hamlet,"
	"King," "Father," "Royal Dane."
	
	                        O, answer me!
	Let me not burst in ignorance, but tell
	Why thy canonized bones, hearsèd in death,
	Have burst their cerements; why the sepulcher,
	Wherein we saw thee quietly interred,
	Hath oped his ponderous and marble jaws
	To cast thee up again.
	
	                What may this mean
	That thou, dead corse, again in complete steel,
	Revisits thus the glimpses of the moon,
	Making night hideous, and we fools of nature
	So horridly to shake our disposition
	With thoughts beyond the reaches of our souls?
	Say, why is this? Wherefore? What should we do?
		canonized: buried according to the canons of the church
		cerements: burial garments
		sepulcher: a burial vault
		interred: buried
		
		steel: indicates that the Ghost is dressed for battle

	SPEECH 3: 2.2.318–32	
Grappling with the suspicion that his father might have been murdered and that his mother might now be married to the murderer, Hamlet expresses an overwhelming emptiness.	I have of late, but wherefore I know not, lost all my mirth, forgone all custom of exercises, and, indeed, it goes so heavily with my disposition that this goodly frame, the earth, seems to me a sterile promontory; this most excellent canopy, the air, look you, this brave o'erhanging firmament, this majestical roof, fretted with golden fire—why, it appeareth nothing to me but a foul and pestilent congregation of vapors. What a piece of work is a man, how noble in reason,how infinite in faculties, in form and moving how express and admirable; in action how like an angel, in apprehension how like a god: the beauty of the world, the paragon of animals—and yet, to me, what is this quintessence of dust? man delights not me; no, nor woman neither, though by your smiling you seem to say so.	**mirth:** joy **promontory:** a cliff jutting into the sea **firmament:** sky **fretted:** adorned **faculties:** abilities **apprehension:** understanding **paragon:** a model of excellence **quintessence:** the purest form

continued on next page

Handout 5.2

	SPEECH 4: 2.2.611–34	
Hamlet harshly criticizes himself for failing to act on behalf of the Ghost's command for revenge.	This is most brave, That I, the son of a dear father murdered, Prompted to my revenge by heaven and hell, Must, like a whore, unpack my heart with words And fall a-cursing like a very drab, A scullion! Fie upon't! Foh! About, my brains!—	**drab:** prostitute **scullion:** kitchen servant

Recognizing the power of art and theater to make us see ourselves in the actions of others, Hamlet will have the players adapt a popular play by adding details told to him by the Ghost to the murder scene.	Hum, I have heard
	That guilty creatures sitting at a play
	Have, by the very cunning of the scene,
	Been struck so to the soul that presently
	They have proclaimed their malefactions.
	For murder, though it have no tongue, will speak
	With most miraculous organ.
	
	        I'll have these players
	Play something like the murder of my father
	Before mine uncle. I'll observe his looks;
	I'll tent him to the quick. If he do blench,
	I know my course.
	
	        The spirit that I have seen
	May be a devil, and the devil hath power
	T' assume a pleasing shape; yea, and perhaps,
	Out of my weakness and my melancholy,
	As he is very potent with such spirits,
	Abuses me to damn me. I'll have grounds
	More relative than this. The play's the thing
	Wherein I'll catch the conscience of the King.
		cunning: art, skill
		
		malefactions: crimes
		
		tent: probe, search
		blench: flinch
		
		melancholy: sadness or depression

continued on next page

Handout 5.2

	SPEECH 5: 3.1.64–96	
Hamlet struggles with questions of life and death and wonders if it is better to suffer and go on living or to oppose the powerful sources of trouble and perhaps die in the process.	To be or not to be—that is the question: Whether 'tis nobler in the mind to suffer The slings and arrows of outrageous fortune, Or to take arms against a sea of troubles, And, by opposing, end them. To die, to sleep— No more—and by a sleep to say we end The heartaches and the thousand natural shocks That flesh is heir to—'tis a consummation Devoutly to be wished. To die, to sleep— To sleep, perchance to dream. Ay, there's the rub, For in that sleep of death what dreams may come, When we have shuffled off this mortal coil, Must give us pause.	**fortune:** bad luck **consummation:** ending **rub:** the catch or problem **mortal coil:** human flesh
As bad as life can be, Hamlet reasons, death is a greater mystery and so we keep on living.	There's the respect That makes calamity of so long life. For who would bear the whips and scorns of time, Th' oppressor's wrong, the proud man's contumely, The pangs of despised love, the law's delay, The insolence of office, and the spurns That patient merit of th' unworthy takes, When he himself might his quietus make With a bare bodkin? Who would fardels bear, To grunt and sweat under a weary life,	**calamity:** disaster **contumely:** arrogance **insolence:** disrespect **spurns:** rejections **quietus:** ending **bodkin:** sharp instrument **fardels:** heavy burdens
	But that the dread of something after death, The undiscovered country from whose bourn No traveler returns, puzzles the will And makes us rather bear those ills we have Than fly to others that we know not of? Thus conscience does make cowards of us all,	**bourn:** boundary **conscience:** thinking, consciousness
Thinking obstructs action.	And thus the native hue of resolution Is sicklied o'er with the pale cast of thought, And enterprises of great pitch and moment With this regard their currents turn awry, And lose the name of action.	**resolution:** action **awry:** off course

Handout 5.3. Hearing the Cinematic

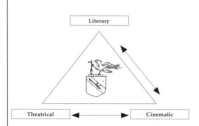

A Focused Listening Guide

1. What mood does the music create? What specifically about the music accomplishes this mood?

2. Describe the tempo of the piece. Is it fast, medium, or slow? Is it constant, or does it change? What effect does the tempo have on the meaning and mood of the piece?

3. What do you notice about the volume?

4. What instruments do you recognize in the piece? Why might the composer have chosen these particular instruments?

5. What effect(s) does the vocals (if any) have on the piece?

6. How do the lyrics contribute to the mood and meaning of the piece?

7. Is there a repeating sound or idea in the music or lyrics? What effect does this repetition have on the piece?

Handout 5.4. Shakespeare's Triangle: Emphasis on Film

Literary: Characters, setting, conflict, language, tone, point of view, mood, symbols, purpose, message, theme, audience/reader

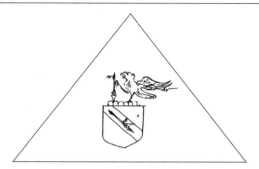

Theatrical: Actors, acting, (voice, facial expression, gesture, movement), costumes, makeup, sets, props, lights, sound, audience

Cinematic: Cameras (shots, angles, densely detailed framing, focus, movement), editing, realistic locations and sets, lighting, sound, special effects, titles, and intertitles, animation, audience/viewer

Cinematic

- How do the <u>camera shots</u>—long, medium, close-up, etc.—establish a sense of connection or disconnection between film characters? Between film viewers and characters?

- How do the <u>camera angles</u>—low, high, eye-level, tilted, etc.—influence a positive or negative interpretation of characters, sets, or action?

- How do the <u>camera movements</u>—pans, tilts, zooms, etc.—and <u>editing techniques</u>—cuts, fades, dissolves, crosscuts, flash cuts, eye-line matches, etc.—contribute to the tempo and style of the scene?

- How does the arrangement of shots—the <u>shot sequence</u>—contribute to the narrative structure and purpose of the scene?

- How does the <u>location</u> affect the scene? How do <u>objects</u> and <u>visual details</u> symbolize ideas?

- How do <u>lighting</u>, <u>color</u>, and <u>special effects</u> create meaning and mood?

- How does the <u>sound design</u>—vocal, environmental, music, silence—intensify or change the images and words?

Reading Shakespeare Film First by Mary Ellen Dakin © 2012 NCTE.

Handout 6.1. Focused Viewing

Film clip title:	
The Three Faces of Shakespeare on Film	**Your focus:**
Literary ■ Who are the <u>characters</u>? Based on what they say, what they do, and what others say about them, what character traits do they embody? ■ When and where is the <u>setting</u>? ■ What happens? Summarize the <u>conflict</u>. ■ How significant is the <u>language</u>? Write down one great line! ■ What is the vocal <u>tone</u> of the dialogue? ■ From whose <u>point of view</u> is the story told? What secondary viewpoints are developed? ■ Who is the <u>intended audience</u>? ■ What is the <u>mood</u>? ■ What objects function as <u>symbols</u>? ■ What is the director's <u>purpose</u>? ■ What issues and ideas seem important? What is the <u>message</u> or <u>theme</u>?	
Theatrical ■ How do the <u>actors</u> interpret the characters they play? What character traits do they emphasize? ■ How do the <u>costumes</u> and <u>makeup</u> reinforce the acting? ■ Describe the main <u>set</u> and the most interesting <u>props</u>.	
Cinematic ■ Describe the <u>photography</u>—camera **shots**, **angles**, and **movement;** lens **focus**. If the norm is a stationary, eye-level, medium shot, note exceptions to the norm. Do patterns emerge? ■ Track the <u>shot sequence</u>: are shots related in a cause-effect pattern or do some shots seem disconnected? ■ Describe <u>editing</u> techniques besides the common cut. Do patterns emerge? ■ How does the <u>sound</u> design (vocal, environmental, music, silence) express and intensify the story? ■ How are <u>lighting</u> and <u>color</u> used to create meaning and mood?	

Reading Shakespeare Film First by Mary Ellen Dakin © 2012 NCTE.

Handout 6.2. Focus on Literature: Characterization

Shakespeare in Love: A Screenplay. Marc Norman and Tom Stoppard
Shakespeare in Love. 1998. Directed by John Madden

How does the director use cinematic and theatrical elements to illustrate literary elements?
—John Golden, "Literature into Film (and Back Again)"

Literary
How do *you* read and interpret a **character**? Locate two places in the screenplay where your character's words and actions reveal something about him or her. Then name two character traits that are illustrated in the text (for example, *calculating, charismatic, cruel, gentle, greedy, hopeful, protective, romantic, ruthless, vain . . .*). Include page #s.

Henslowe	Fennyman	Will	Viola	Nurse	Sir Robert	Lord Wessex	Urchin

Literary Evidence: Your character's words and/or actions . . .	. . . suggest that he or she is (name two character traits):
1. On p. 39, Nurse covers up for Viola's disguise by telling Will, "Master Kent is my nephew."	1. Clever and Protective
2. On p. 41, after Viola admits her love for Master Shakespeare, Nurse firmly warns, "My lady, this play will end badly. I will tell," but she doesn't tell, and she helps Viola to better disguise herself as a boy actor.	2. Loyal

Theatrical	**Cinematic**
How does the **actor** illustrate the **character**? How does the acting (line delivery, facial expressions, actions and gestures) help? How do costumes, makeup, sets, and props help?	How does the **director** illustrate the **character**? How do the camera work (shots, angles, focus, movement), editing, location, lighting, sound (vocal, environmental, music, silence) help?
Her <u>costume</u>, especially the headpiece she wears, makes her look like a nun, and even when she is in the theater with the aristocrats, her costume is like a servant's. The <u>actor</u> looks grandmotherly—older and heavier. She <u>delivers her lines</u> with a worried tone, as if she is having second thoughts every time she speaks. She fusses over Viola—even though the script describes her helping Viola dress and clean herself, seeing Nurse <u>act</u> this out emphasizes her protective character.	When Viola appears at the comedy performed for the Queen, the camera shows Lord Wessex looking at Viola. Viola doesn't notice but Nurse does. Using 3 <u>separation shots</u>, the camera focuses on Wessex looking at Viola, then Nurse looking at Wessex with worry, then back to moody Wessex, who only sees Viola. This shows Nurse is protective but, more than clever, she is observant and perceptive. These camera shots foreshadow a triangle of trouble.

Handout 6.3. Focus on Literature

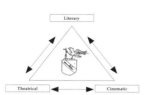

How does the director use cinematic and theatrical elements to illustrate literary elements?
— John Golden, "Literature into Film (and Back Again)"

Literary Elements
In this scene, how do *you* read and interpret the (*choose one*) **characters / setting / conflict / language / tone / point of view / audience / mood / symbols / author's purpose / message and themes?**

The literary evidence (words, actions):	**...supports my reading because it shows that:**
1.	1.
2.	2.

Theatrical and Cinematic Elements	How do these cinematic and theatrical elements help to illustrate the literary element?

Reading Shakespeare Film First by Mary Ellen Dakin © 2012 NCTE.

Handout 6.4. Transmediation: Reading Shakespeare as Literary, Theatrical, and Cinematic Text

Together we have learned to read Shakespeare as great literature, as a working script for theater, and as the blueprint for something that didn't exist when Shakespeare lived—the medium of film.

Act 1
Read a passage from a play by Shakespeare and annotate the text for the literary elements of characters, setting, conflict, language, tone, mood, symbols, purposes, and themes.

Act 2
Assume the role of filmmaker. Because most films do not exceed two hours, edit Shakespeare's script by *at least 50 percent*. What dialogue is essential to a modern audience's understanding of the characters and conflict? Cut the rest.

Act 3
Look closely at what you have cut—how can you put it back in? What theatrical and cinematic elements can you use to illustrate and interpret the words you have kept? What theatrical and cinematic elements can you use to translate into images and sound the words you have cut? Write in the margins descriptive directorial commentary that explains your answers.

Act 4
View the scene on film, keeping notes during the first viewing on the theatrical elements you see and hear in the film adaptation of Shakespeare's text. If possible, before the second viewing read the screenplay adaptation of the scene, marking the deletions and changes the director and writer made to Shakespeare's text. View the scene a second time, keeping notes on the cinematic elements you see and hear.

Act 5
Synthesize your triple reading into a written response or presentation:

> How does the filmmaker translate the literary elements of the passage—the characters, setting, conflict, language, tone, mood, symbols, purposes, and themes—using theatrical and cinematic elements? What is lost and what is gained in translation?

Reading Shakespeare Film First by Mary Ellen Dakin © 2012 NCTE.

Handout 7.1. *Henry V* Viewing Guide

Henry V Directed by Kenneth Branagh	Act 1 Viewing Guide

Part 1: DVD Chapter 2 to Chapter 8. Approximate time, 15 minutes.
WHILE VIEWING:

Make notes here of any vivid visual images you notice:

Make notes here of any vivid sounds (vocal, environmental, music, silence) you notice:

AFTER VIEWING PART 1 OF THE FILM:
What is the effect of the location change from the soundstage where Chorus, played by Derek Jacobi, speaks the Prologue to the set of the first scene?

How do theatrical elements (acting, costumes, makeup, props, lighting, color) establish differences between King Henry V, played by Kenneth Branagh, and the other characters?

Which character do you most like or dislike? What theatrical or cinematic elements contribute to your feelings?

How do the lighting and the use of color (or the absence of color) contribute to the mood?

How does King Henry V deal with conflict in act 1 of the film? What character traits does he display?

continued on next page

Handout 7.1

| *Henry V*
Directed by Kenneth Branagh | **Act 2 Viewing Guide** |

Part 2: DVD Chapter 9 to Chapter 13. Approximate time, 20 minutes.
WHILE VIEWING:

Make notes here of any vivid visual images you notice:

Make notes here of any vivid sounds (vocal, environmental, music, silence) you notice:

AFTER VIEWING PART 2 OF THE FILM:
In what ways is the location for Chorus's second speech different in space and time from the location in act 1?

What three tone words would you use to describe Branagh's line delivery at the beginning, middle, and end of the scene in which he confronts the three traitors? What does Branagh's line delivery in this scene reveal about his understanding of Henry V as a man and as a leader?

In the scene in which Henry confronts the traitors, how do the camera shots and framing reinforce the themes of loyalty and betrayal?

In contrast to the traitors' scene, what does the camera contribute to the scene in which the heartbroken Hostess of the tavern relates the death of Falstaff?

In the scene that introduces the French royal court, what theatrical and cinematic techniques contribute to the tension?

How is lighting used throughout act 2 to dramatize characters, sets, and mood?

continued on next page

Handout 7.1	

Henry V Directed by Kenneth Branagh	**Act 3 Viewing Guide**

Part 3: DVD Chapter 14 to Chapter 21. Approximate time, 18 minutes.
WHILE VIEWING:

> Make notes here of any vivid visual images you notice:

> Make notes here of any vivid sounds (vocal, environmental, music, silence) you notice:

AFTER VIEWING PART 3 OF THE FILM:
What are the most significant differences, theatrically and cinematically, between the scene of Chorus's third speech and the scenes of his first two?

What is the director's interpretation of Henry's siege of Harfleur—hellish or heroic? What images and sounds support your opinion?

What is the effect of hearing French spoken in the scene between Princess Katherine and her Gentlewoman? What is the point of Katherine's playful lesson in learning English names for parts of the human body? How does the mood shift at the end of the scene?

Describe the wordless montage of images and sounds that dramatizes the aftermath of Henry's victory at Harfleur. What story does the montage tell?

In Shakespeare's play, Captain Fluellen tells King Henry of Bardolph's imminent execution for robbing a French church; Henry briefly expresses support for the execution, which takes place off-stage. What does this film production add to your understanding of Henry's character? What does the on-camera hanging of Bardolph contribute to themes of loyalty, mercy, and justice?

Immediately following the grisly hanging of one of his own men, how does the sequence and separation of shots between Henry and the French Herald help to reestablish respect and sympathy for Henry?

continued on next page

Handout 7.1

Henry V Directed by Kenneth Branagh	Act 4 Viewing Guide

Part 4: DVD Chapter 27 to Chapter 32. Approximate time, 32 minutes.
WHILE VIEWING:

> Make notes here of any vivid visual images you notice:

> Make notes here of any vivid sounds (vocal, environmental, music, silence) you notice:

AFTER VIEWING PART 4 OF THE FILM:

On the morning of battle, the scene begins with shots of the French army at right-screen, then shots of the English army at left-screen. What theatrical elements (costumes, makeup, facial expressions, etc.) and cinematic elements (camera shots and framing, camera angles, location, light, sound) establish a stark contrast between the two camps before the battle begins?

What is the effect of Henry's St. Crispin's Day speech on the demoralized and vastly outnumbered English soldiers? What do the camera shots and angles, lighting, color, and sound design contribute to the effect of the speech?

Throughout this film production, the minor character of the French Herald assumes greater significance. Describe the relationship that develops throughout this scene between the English King and the French Herald.

Much of the battle scene is filmed as a wordless montage of camera shots, camera angles, slow-motion photography, camera movement, graphic visual images, music, and a dramatic confusion of sounds. What does this montage contribute to the theme of honor and heroism?

How is the slaughter of the English boys dramatized?

At the end of the battle, when Herald reports the numbers of the dead to King Henry, describe the tones of the music that begins with the diegetic sound of a single soldier's voice and ends with the nondiegetic sound of an orchestra. Does the sound track reinforce or contradict the images?

continued on next page

Handout 7.1

Henry V Directed by Kenneth Branagh	Act 5 Viewing Guide

Part 5: DVD Chapter 33 to Chapter 35. Approximate time, 16 minutes.
WHILE VIEWING:

Make notes here of any vivid visual images you notice:

Make notes here of any vivid sounds (vocal, environmental, music, silence) you notice:

AFTER VIEWING PART 5 OF THE FILM:
How does the framing of the long opening shot reflect the troubled history between England and France?

What is the purpose of the series of flashbacks during the Duke of Burgundy's speech about the suffering of France?

A half-lit face can suggest internal division or duplicity; a face lit from the front can suggest openness, honesty, and goodness. What does the lighting of Henry's and Katherine's faces in this scene suggest about their characters?

The sounds of the English and French languages intertwine as Henry attempts to communicate his love to Katherine. How sincere is Henry's expression of love as a prerequisite to their marriage? What freedom of choice does Katherine have? How does the acting of Branagh and Emma Thompson (line delivery, facial expression, gesture, movement) influence your understanding of each character?

How would you describe the tone of Chorus's Epilogue? What theatrical and cinematic elements contribute to the actor Derek Jacobi's performance?

For final reflection: Is this a film that glorifies war?

Handout 7.2. Shot Sequence Analysis

Number the shots in a sequence and sketch the contents of a key frame in each shot. Write notes for each shot that describe the characters, action, and dialogue: the approximate shot length in seconds; the camera shot, angle, or movement; the action, lighting, sound, or transitions between shots.

Shot 1:

Shot 2:

Shot 3:

Shot 4:

Shot 5, *continued on new sheet as needed*

Reading Shakespeare Film First by Mary Ellen Dakin © 2012 NCTE.

Handout 8.1. Transmediating Shakespeare Production Project Calendar

Inside Outsiders

Day 1	Day 2	Day 3	Day 4	Day 5
▶ Focus Question ▶ Context Chart 8.2 ▶ Graphic Maps 8.3 ▶ Project Handout 8.4	▶ Scene Scripts 8.5 ▶ Teams form and choose 3 scenes to read in reciprocal teaching roles	▶ Reading selected scenes and reciprocal teaching concludes. ▶ Character Chart 8.6–8.7 ▶ Teams select one scene.	▶ Focused viewing of the documentary model, *Looking for Richard* ▶ Project Role Sheet 8.8	Stage 1 begins: ▶ Read and research Shakespeare's scene.
Day 6	**Day 7**	**Day 8**	**Day 9**	**Day 10**
Stage 1 continues: ▶ Storyboard the scene for a film performance, 8.9.	Stage 2 begins: ▶ Direct and rehearse the scene.	Stage 2 continues: ▶ Perform and film the scene, guided by storyboard. ▶ Interview experts.	Stage 2 continues: ▶ Perform, film, interview	Stage 2 continues and concludes.
Day 11	**Day 12**	**Day 13**	**Day 14**	**Day 15**
Stage 3 begins: ▶ Teams view raw footage. ▶ Storyboard footage into a documentary of the process.	Stage 3 continues: ▶ Assemble rough cuts. ▶ Establish assessment criteria: read film reviews, view anchor videos.	Stage 3 continues: ▶ Assemble final cuts. ▶ Establish assessment criteria, 8.10.	Stage 3 concludes: ▶ Title, transition, and music cuts ▶ Construct project rubric, 8.11.	▶ Film Festival! ▶ Final Reflection 8.12

Reading Shakespeare Film First by Mary Ellen Dakin © 2012 NCTE.

Handout 8.2. Inside Outsiders Context Chart

Each scene focuses on a character who inhabits the realms of power in the play but who was either born outside the inner circles of power or is driven out.

Welcome to the world of . . . ■ Katherine, the shrew ■ Caliban, the enslaved native ■ Shylock, the Jew ■ Hermione, the accused adulteress ■ Othello, the Moor ■ Edmund, the bastard ■ Viola, the young woman disguised as a boy	**From *The Taming of the Shrew* 4.5, 5.5** When Petruchio arrives in Padua, he learns that the wealthy Baptista is eager to marry off his older shrewish daughter. Using wit and reverse psychology, Petruchio charms **Katherine** the shrew into marriage. At the wedding, he slaps the priest, drags her home, and deprives her of food and proper clothing; he even wagers with other men that his wife is now more obedient than theirs. . . .	**From *The Tempest* 1.2** Prospero, Duke of Milan, is betrayed and cast adrift in a rotting boat with his books of magic and 3-year-old daughter, Miranda. They survive and arrive at an island inhabited by a spirit, Ariel, and one person, **Caliban**, the son of Sycorax, a witch banished from Algiers and abandoned pregnant on the island by sailors. At first, Prospero is kind to Caliban, but years later, seeing him as a threat to Miranda, he enslaves him. . . .
From *The Merchant of Venice* 3.1 News has just reached Venice that a Christian merchant named Antonio is bankrupt. At the same time, a Jewish moneylender, **Shylock**, learns that his daughter has stolen gold and jewels from him and eloped with Antonio's friend. Earlier in the play, Antonio had taken a loan from Shylock and agreed to repay it in full or forfeit a pound of his flesh. . . .	**From *The Winter's Tale* 2.1, 3.2** After a 9-month visit, King Polixenes tells his friend King Leontes that he must return home. Leontes unsuccessfully begs Polixenes to stay, but when his pregnant wife **Hermione** asks, Polixenes agrees. Suddenly jealous, Leontes plots the murder of his friend but Polixenes escapes. Now he confronts his innocent, pregnant Queen. . . .	**From *Othello* 1.1, 1.2** Overlooked for an army promotion, Iago plots his revenge on **Othello**, a black Moor who serves the Duke of Venice. Knowing that Desdemona, the daughter of a powerful Venetian senator named Brabantio, has just eloped with Othello, Iago rudely alarms the senator, then hurries back to Othello, feigning loyalty to the general he now despises. . . .
From *King Lear* 1.1, 1.2 As Kent and Gloucester discuss King Lear's plans to divide the kingdom among his three daughters, Gloucester introduces his illegitimate son, **Edmund**, to Kent. When the older men leave, Edmund questions his status and compares himself to his brother and his father's legitimate son, Edgar. . . .	**From *Twelfth Night* 1.2** Separated from her twin brother Sebastian during a shipwreck, **Viola** finds herself washed ashore with the Sea Captain and sailors in a foreign land. In grief for her drowned brother and concerned for her safety, Viola decides to disguise herself as a eunuch and to serve the duke Orsino. . . .	**Focus Questions** 1. What causes each character to be perceived as different, dangerous, or despised? 2. What effect does their outsider status have on each character? How does each character respond?

Reading Shakespeare Film First by Mary Ellen Dakin © 2012 NCTE.

Handout 8.3. Graphic Maps

Graphic Map of William Shakespeare's *The Taming of the Shrew,* drawn by Jennifer Sao

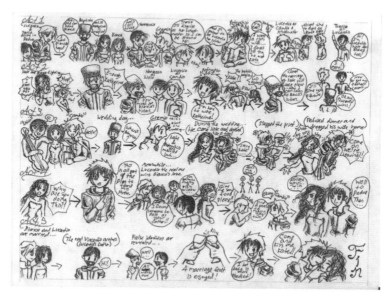

Graphic Map of William Shakespeare's *The Tempest,* drawn by Jennifer Sao

continued on next page

Handout 8.3

Graphic Map of William Shakespeare's *The Merchant of Venice,* drawn by Jennifer Sao

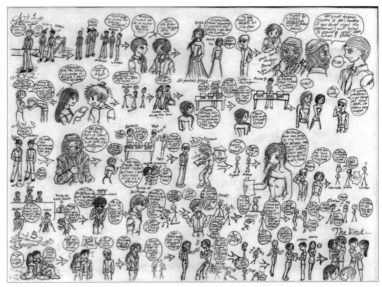

Graphic Map of William Shakespeare's *The Winter's Tale,* drawn by Jennifer Sao

continued on next page

Handout 8.3

Graphic Map of William Shakespeare's *Othello,* drawn by Jennifer Sao

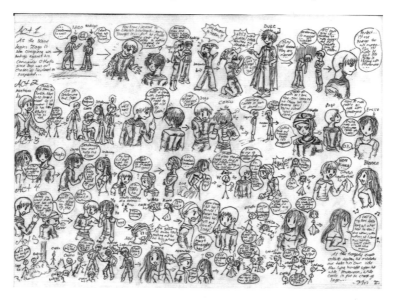

Graphic Map of William Shakespeare's *King Lear,* drawn by Jennifer Sao

continued on next page

Handout 8.3

Graphic Map of William Shakespeare's *Twelfth Night*, drawn by Jennifer Sao

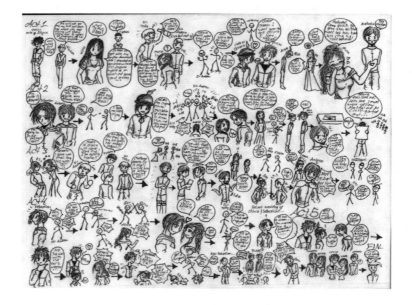

Handout 8.4. Final Production Project: Transmediating Shakespeare

Transmediation is a young English word made from the ancient Latin roots, *trans-* meaning "across" and *medius* meaning "middle." Today we use the word to name the act of translating meaning from one sign system into another. When we transmediate literature into theater and film, words on a page become sounds and images, sentences and scenes become shot sequences. We invent, in the words of *Hamlet* film director Michael Almereyda, "a parallel visual language that might hold a candle to Shakespeare's poetry."

Ask Questions

In his documentary film, *Looking for Richard*, Al Pacino asks, "What gets between us and Shakespeare?" This project challenges us to pile twenty-first-century communication tools in the space between us and Shakespeare's text and to question whether we are moving closer to or further from Shakespeare. When we transmediate the literary elements of a Shakespeare scene into a theatrical and cinematic production, what is lost in translation? What is gained? How should we read Shakespeare in the twenty-first century?

This project challenges you to find answers to these essential questions, and to ask more questions of your own.

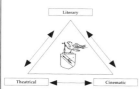

Search for Answers

You will work in companies of five, reading several short scenes from a collection of scripts excerpted from William Shakespeare's plays. In this collection, each scene focuses on a character who is pushed to the edges of the world in which he or she lives and marked by those more powerful as different, dangerous, and even despised. Some of the issues that get between us—race, religion, gender, ethnicity, age, education, wealth, and social status—are issues that divide them too.

View the Model

View *Looking for Richard* and take focused notes on the cinematic composition.

Walk the Triangle

The project will be completed in three stages. Film each stage in the process.

> **Stage One**: Read, Reread, Research
> **Stage Two**: Interview, Rehearse, Storyboard, Perform
> **Stage Three**: View, Storyboard, Edit, Produce, Assess, Reflect

During each stage, each member of your team will assume primary responsibility for a specific role. Work together, not apart: never forget that you are a team.

Stage 1: Literary Roles	Stage 2: Theatrical Roles	Stage 3: Cinematic Roles
Discussion leader Director Readers Camera operator	Director Actors Interviewer Camera operator	Director Editor

Reading Shakespeare Film First by Mary Ellen Dakin © 2012 NCTE.

Handout 8.5. Themed Excerpts: Inside Outsiders

These scenes focus on characters who inhabit the realms of power in the play but were either born outside the inner circles of power or are driven out: Katherine the Shrew, Caliban the enslaved native, Shylock the Jew, Hermione the accused adulteress, Othello the Moor, Edmund the bastard, and Viola the young woman disguised as a boy in a foreign place.

From *The Taming of the Shrew* 4.5, 5.2
Speaking Parts: 4

Enter PETRUCHIO, KATHERINE,
HORTENSIO, and Servants
PETRUCHIO
Come on, i' God's name, once more toward our father's.
Good Lord, how bright and goodly shines the moon!
KATHERINE
The moon? The sun! It is not moonlight now.
PETRUCHIO
I say it is the moon that shines so bright.
KATHERINE
I know it is the sun that shines so bright.
PETRUCHIO
Now, by my mother's son, and that's myself,
It shall be moon, or star, or what I list,
Or e'er I journey to your father's house.
[*To Servants.*] Go on, and fetch our horses back again. –
Evermore crossed and crossed, nothing but crossed!
HORTENSIO [*to Katherine*]
Say as he says, or we shall never go.
KATHERINE
Forward, I pray, since we have come so far,
And be it moon, or sun, or what you please.
And if you please to call it a rush candle,
Henceforth I vow it shall be so for me.
PETRUCHIO
I say it is the moon.
KATHERINE
I know it is the moon.
PETRUCHIO
Nay, then you lie. It is the blessèd sun.

KATHERINE
Then God be blest, it is the blessed sun.
But sun it is not, when you say it is not,
And the moon changes even as your mind.
What you will have it named, even that it is,
And so it shall be so for Katherine.
Exit.

HORTENSIO
Petruchio, go thy ways, the field is won…

PETRUCHIO
Nay, I will win my wager better yet,
And show more sign of her obedience,
Her new-built virtue and obedience.

Enter KATHERINE, BIANCA, and WIDOW

See where she comes, and brings your froward wives
As prisoners to her womanly persuasion. –
Katherine, that cap of yours becomes you not.
Off with that bauble, throw it underfoot…
[*She obeys.*]
Katherine, I charge thee tell these headstrong women
What duty they do owe their lords and husbands.
WIDOW
Come, come, you're mocking. We will have no telling.
PETRUCHIO
Come on, I say, and first begin with her.
WIDOW She shall not.
PETRUCHIO
I say she shall. – And first begin with her.

continued on next page

Handout 8.5

KATHERINE

Fie, fie! Unknit that threat'ning unkind brow,
And dart not scornful glances from those eyes
To wound thy lord, thy king, thy governor…
Thy husband is thy lord, thy life, thy keeper,
Thy head, thy sovereign, one that cares for thee,
And for thy maintenance commits his body
To painful labor both by sea and land,
To watch the night in storms, the day in cold,
Whilst thou liest warm at home, secure and safe,
And craves no other tribute at thy hands
But love, fair looks, and true obedience –
Too little payment for so great a debt.
Such duty as the subject owes the prince,
Even such a woman oweth to her husband;
And when she is froward, peevish, sullen, sour,
And not obedient to his honest will,
What is she but a foul contending rebel
And graceless traitor to her loving lord?
I am ashamed that women are so simple
To offer war where they should kneel for peace,
Or seek for rule, supremacy, and sway
When they are bound to serve, love, and obey.
Why are our bodies soft and weak and smooth,
Unapt to toil and trouble in the world,
But that our soft conditions and our hearts
Should well agree with our external parts?
Come, come, you froward and unable worms!
My mind hath been as big as one of yours,
My heart as great, my reason haply more,
To bandy word for word and frown for frown;
But now I see our lances are but straws,
Our strength as weak, our weakness past compare,

That seeming to be most which we indeed least are.
Then vail your stomachs, for it is no boot,
And place your hands below your husband's foot;
In token of which duty, if he please,
My hand is ready, may it do him ease.
PETRUCHIO
Why, there's a wench! Come on, and kiss me, Kate.

[*They kiss.*]

From *The Tempest* 1.2
Speaking Parts: 4

PROSPERO We'll visit Caliban, my slave, who never
Yields us kind answer.
MIRANDA [*rising*] 'Tis a villain, sir,
I do not love to look on.
PROSPERO But, as 'tis,
We cannot miss him. He does make our fire,
Fetch in our wood, and serves in offices
That profit us. – What ho, slave, Caliban!
Thou earth, thou, speak!
CALIBAN [*within*] There's wood enough within.
PROSPERO
Come forth, I say. There's other business for thee.
Come, thou tortoise. When?

Enter ARIEL like a water nymph.

Fine apparition! My quaint Ariel,
Hark in thine ear.   [*He whispers to Ariel.*]
ARIEL My lord, it shall be done. *He exits.*
PROSPERO [*to Caliban*]
Thou poisonous slave, got by the devil himself
Upon thy wicked dam, come forth!

continued on next page

Handout 8.5

Enter CALIBAN

CALIBAN
As wicked dew as e'er my mother brushed
With raven's feather from unwholesome fen
Drop on you both. A southwest blow on you
And blister you all o'er.
PROSPERO
For this, be sure, tonight thou shalt have
cramps,
Side-stitches that shall pen thy breath up.
Urchins
Shall forth at vast of night that they may
work
All exercise on thee. Thou shalt be pinched
As thick as honeycomb, each pinch more
stinging
Than bees that made 'em.
CALIBAN   I must eat my dinner.
This island's mine by Sycorax, my mother,
Which thou tak'st from me. When thou
cam'st first,
Thou strok'st me and made much of me,
wouldst give me
Water with berries in't, and teach me how
To name the bigger light and how the less,
That burn by day and night. And then I
loved thee,
And showed thee all the qualities o' th' isle,
The fresh springs, brine pits, barren place
and fertile.
Cursed be I that did so! All the charms
Of Sycorax, toads, beetles, bats, light on you,
For I am all the subjects that you have,
Which first was mine own king; and here
you sty me
In this hard rock, whiles you do keep from
me
The rest o' th' island.
PROSPERO   Thou most lying slave,
Whom stripes may move, not kindness, I
have used thee,
Filth as thou art, with humane care, and
lodged thee
In mine own cell, till thou didst seek to violate
The honor of my child.

CALIBAN
O ho, O ho! Would't had been done!
Thou didst prevent me. I had peopled else
This isle with Calibans.
MIRANDA   Abhorrèd slave,
Which any print of goodness wilt not take,
Being capable of all ill! I pitied thee,
Took pains to make thee speak, taught thee
each hour
One thing or other. When thou didst not,
savage,
Know thine own meaning, but wouldst
gabble like
A thing most brutish, I endowed thy
purposes
With words that made them known. But
thy vile race,
Though thou didst learn, had that in 't which
good natures
Could not abide to be with. Therefore wast
thou
Deservedly confined into this rock,
Who hadst deserved more than a prison.
CALIBAN
You taught me language, and my profit on 't
Is I know how to curse. The red plague rid
you
For learning me your language!
PROSPERO   Hagseed, hence!
Fetch us in fuel; and be quick…Shrugg'st
thou, malice?
If thou neglect'st or dost unwillingly
What I command, I'll rack thee with old
cramps,
Fill all thy bones with aches, make thee roar
That beasts shall tremble at thy din.
CALIBAN   No, pray thee.
[*Aside.*] I must obey. His art is of such
power
It would control my dam's god, Setebos,
And make a vassal of him.
PROSPERO   So, slave, hence.
Caliban exits.

continued on next page

Handout 8.5

From *The Merchant of Venice* **Act 3.1**
Speaking parts: 4

Enter SOLANIO and SALARINO

SOLANIO
Now, what news on the Rialto?
SALARINO
Why, yet it lives there unchecked that Antonio hath a ship of rich lading wracked on the Narrow Seas – the Goodwins, I think they call the place – a very dangerous flat, and fatal, where the carcasses of many a tall ship lie buried…
SOLANIO
But it is true…that the good Antonio, the honest Antonio – O, that I had a title good enough to keep his name company! –
SALARINO
Come, the full stop.
SOLANIO
Ha, what sayest thou? Why, the end is, he hath lost a ship.
SALARINO
I would it might prove the end of his losses.
SOLANIO
Let me say "amen" betimes, lest the devil cross my prayer, for here he comes in the likeness of a Jew.

Enter SHYLOCK
How now, Shylock, what news among the merchants?
SHYLOCK
You knew, none so well, none so well as you, of my daughter's flight.
SALARINO
That's certain. I for my part knew the tailor that made the wings she flew withal.
SOLANIO
And Shylock for his own part knew the bird was fledge, and then it is the complexion of them all to leave the dam.
SHYLOCK
She is damned for it.

SALARINO
That's certain, if the devil may be her judge.
SHYLOCK
My own flesh and blood to rebel!...
SALARINO
There is more difference between thy flesh and hers than between jet and ivory, more between your bloods than there is between red wine and Rhenish. But tell us, do you hear whether Antonio have had any loss at sea or no?
SHYLOCK
There I have another bad match! A bankrout, a prodigal, who dare scarce show his head on the Rialto, a beggar that was used to come so smug upon the mart! Let him look to his bond. He was wont to call me usurer; let him look to his bond. He was wont to lend money for a Christian cur'sy; let him look to his bond.
SALARINO
Why, I am sure if he forfeit, thou wilt not take his flesh! What's that good for?
SHYLOCK
To bait fish withal; if it will feed nothing else, it will feed my revenge. He hath disgraced me and hindered me half a million, laughed at my losses, mocked at my gains, scorned my nation, thwarted my bargains, cooled my friends, heated mine enemies – and what's his reason? I am a Jew. Hath not a Jew eyes? Hath not a Jew hands, organs, dimensions, senses, affections, passions? Fed with the same food, hurt with the same weapons, subject to the same diseases, healed by the same means, warmed and cooled by the same winter and summer as a Christian is? If you prick us, do we not bleed? If you tickle us, do we not laugh? If you poison us, do we not die? And if you wrong us, shall we not revenge? If we are like you in the rest, we will resemble you in that. If a Jew wrong a Christian, what is his humility? Revenge. If a Christian

continued on next page

Handout 8.5

wrong a Jew, what should his sufferance be by Christian example? Why, revenge! The villainy you teach me I will execute, and it shall go hard but I will better the instruction…

Enter TUBAL

SOLANIO
Here comes another of the tribe; a third cannot be matched unless the devil himself turn Jew.

SALARINO, SOLANIO…exit.

SHYLOCK
How now, Tubal, what news from Genoa? Hast thou found my daughter?
TUBAL
I often came where I did hear of her, but cannot find her.
SHYLOCK
Why, there, there, there, there! A diamond gone cost me two thousand ducats in Frankfort! The curse never fell upon our nation till now, I never felt it till now. Two thousand ducats in that, and other precious, precious jewels! I would my daughter were dead at my foot and the jewels in her ear; would she were hearsed at my foot and the ducats in her coffin…
TUBAL
Yes, other men have ill luck, too. Antonio, as I heard in Genoa – …There came divers of Antonio's creditors in my company to Venice that swear he cannot choose but break.
SHYLOCK
I am very glad of it. I'll plague him, I'll torture him. I am glad of it.
TUBAL
One of them showed me a ring that he had of your daughter for a monkey.
SHYLOCK
Out upon her! Thou torturest me, Tubal. It

was my turquoise! I had it of Leah when I was a bachelor. I would not have given it for a wilderness of monkeys.
TUBAL
But Antonio is certainly undone.
SHYLOCK
Nay, that's true, that's very true. Go, Tubal, fee me an officer. Bespeak him a fortnight before. I will have the heart of him if he forfeit, for were he out of Venice I can make what merchandise I will. Go, Tubal, and meet me at our synagogue. Go, good Tubal, at our synagogue, Tubal.

They exit.

From *The Winter's Tale* 2.1, 3.2
Speaking parts: 5

Enter HERMIONE, MAMILLIUS, and Ladies

HERMIONE
Take the boy to you. He so troubles me
'Tis past enduring…
FIRST LADY
                                    Hark ye,
The Queen your mother rounds apace. We shall
Present our services to a fine new prince
One of these days, and then you'd wanton with us
If we would have you…
HERMIONE
What wisdom stirs amongst you? – Come, sir, now
I am for you again. Pray you sit by us,
And tell 's a tale.
MAMILLIUS
Merry or sad shall 't be?
HERMIONE
As merry as you will.
MAMILLIUS
A sad tale's best for winter. I have one
Of sprites and goblins.

continued on next page

Handout 8.5

HERMIONE
                    Let's have that, good sir.
Come on, sit down. Come on, and do your best
To fright me with your sprites. You're powerful at it...

Enter LEONTES, Lords, and Officers...

LEONTES
[*To Hermione*] Give me the boy. I am glad you did not nurse him.
Though he does bear some signs of me, yet you
Have too much blood in him.
HERMIONE
What is this? Sport?
LEONTES [*to the Ladies*]
Bear the boy hence. He shall not come about her.
Away with him, and let her sport herself
With that she's big with, [*to Hermione*] for 'tis Polixenes
Has made thee swell thus.
                    [*A Lady exits with Mamillius.*]

HERMIONE But I'd say he had not,
And I'll be sworn you would believe my saying,
Howe'er you lean to th' nayward.
LEONTES   You, my lords,
Look on her, mark her well...But be 't known...
She's an adult'ress.
HERMIONE
                    Should a villain say so,
The most replenished villain in the world,
He were as much more villain. You, my lord,
Do but mistake.
LEONTES   You have mistook, my lady,
Polixenes for Leontes. O thou thing,
Which I'll not call a creature of thy place
Lest barbarism, making me the precedent,
Should a like language use to all degrees,

And mannerly distinguishment leave out
Betwixt the prince and beggar. – I have said
She's an adult'ress; I have said with whom.
More, she's a traitor...
A bed-swerver, even as bad as those
That vulgars give bold'st titles; ay, and privy
To this their late escape.
HERMIONE
                    No, by my life,
Privy to none of this...
                    There's some ill planet reigns.
I must be patient till the heavens look
With an aspect more favorable. Good my lords,
I am not prone to weeping, as our sex
Commonly are, the want of which vain dew
Perchance shall dry your pities. But I have
That honorable grief lodged here which burns
Worse than tears drown...
LEONTES
                    Away with her to prison.
He who shall speak for her is afar off guilty
But that he speaks...Read the indictment.

OFFICER
[*reads*] *Hermione, queen to the worthy Leontes, King of Sicilia, thou art here accused and arraigned of high treason, in committing adultery with Polixenes, King of Bohemia, and conspiring with Camillo to take away the life of our sovereign lord the King, thy royal husband...*
HERMIONE
Since what I am to say must be but that
Which contradicts my accusation, and
The testimony on my part no other
But what comes from myself, it shall scarce boot me
To say "Not guilty." Mine integrity,
Being counted falsehood, shall, as I express it,

continued on next page

Handout 8.5

Be so received. But thus: if powers divine
Behold our human actions, as they do,
I doubt not then but innocence shall make
False accusation blush and tyranny
Tremble at patience…Adieu, my lord.
I never wished to see you sorry; now
I trust I shall. – My women, come; you
have leave.
LEONTES
Go, do our bidding. Hence!
*[HERMIONE exits, under guard, with her
Ladies.]*

From *Othello* 1.1, 1.2
Speaking Parts: 4

Enter Roderigo and Iago.
RODERIGO
What ho, Brabantio! Signior Brabantio, ho!
IAGO
Awake! What ho, Brabantio! Thieves,
thieves!
Look to your house, your daughter, and
your bags! Thieves, thieves!
[Enter BRABANTIO] above.

BRABANTIO
What is the reason of this terrible sum-
mons?
What is the matter there?
RODERIGO
Signior, is all your family within?
IAGO
Are your doors locked?
BRABANTIO Why, wherefore ask you
this?
IAGO
Zounds, sir, you're robbed. For shame, put
on your gown!
Your heart is burst. You have lost half your
soul.
Even now, now, very now, an old black ram
Is tupping your white ewe. Arise, arise!

Awake the snorting citizens with the bell,
Or else the devil will make a grandsire of
you.
Arise, I say!
BRABANTIO What, have you lost your
wits?…
What tell'st thou me of robbing? This is
Venice. My house is not a grange…
IAGO
Zounds, sir, you are one of those that will
not serve God if the devil bid you. Because
we come to do you service and you think
we are ruffians, you'll have your daughter
covered with a Barbary horse, you'll have
your nephews neigh to you, you'll have
coursers for cousins and jennets for ger-
mans.
BRABANTIO
What profane wretch art thou?
IAGO
I am one, sir, that comes to tell you your
daughter and the Moor are now making
the beast with two backs…
BRABANTIO
Strike on the tinder, ho!
Give me a taper. Call up all my people.
This accident is not unlike my dream.
Belief of it oppresses me already.
Light, I say, light!
He exits.

IAGO
Farewell, for I must leave you.
It seems not meet nor wholesome to my
place
To be produced…Against the Moor…
Though I do hate him as I do hell pains,
Yet, for necessity of present life,
I must show out a flag and sign of love –
Which is indeed but sign… So, farewell.
He exits.

*Enter BRABANTIO (in his nightgown) with
Servants and Torches.*

continued on next page

Handout 8.5

BRABANTIO
It is too true an evil. Gone she is… Now, Roderigo,
Where didst thou see her? – O unhappy girl! – With the Moor, sayst thou? – Who would be a father? – …
Raise all my kindred. – Are they married, think you?
RODERIGO   Truly, I think they are…
BRABANTIO
Call up my brother. – …Do you know
Where we may apprehend her and the Moor?
RODERIGO
I think I can discover him, if you please
To get good guard and go along with me.
BRABANTIO
Pray you, lead on…
Exeunt

Enter OTHELLO, IAGO, Attendants, with Torches.
IAGO
…Are you fast married? Be assured of this,
That the magnifico is much beloved,
And hath in his effect a voice potential
As double as the Duke's. He will divorce you
Or put upon you what restraint or griev-ance
The law (with all his might to enforce it on)
Will give him cable.
OTHELLO   Let him do his spite.
My services which I have done the signiory
Shall out-tongue his complaints…I fetch my life and being
From men of royal siege, and my demerits
May speak unbonneted to as proud a fortune
As this that I have reached. For know, Iago,
But that I love the gentle Desdemona,
I would not my unhousèd free condition
Put into circumscription and confine

For the sea's worth. But, look, what lights come yond?
IAGO
Those are the raisèd father and his friends.
You were best go in.
OTHELLO   Not I. I must be found.
My parts, my title, and my perfect soul
Shall manifest me rightly. Is it they?
IAGO By Janus, I think no…

Enter BRABANTIO, RODERIGO, with Officers, and Torches…

OTHELLO   Holla, stand there!
RODERIGO   Signior, it is the Moor.
BRABANTIO   Down with him, thief!
      [They draw their swords.]…

OTHELLO
Keep up your bright swords, for the dew will rust them.
Good signior, you shall more command with years
Than with your weapons.
BRABANTIO
O, thou foul thief, where hast thou stowed my daughter?
Damned as thou art, thou hast enchanted her!...
OTHELLO
      Whither will you that I go
To answer this your charge?
BRABANTIO
To prison, till fit time
Of law and course of direct session
Call thee to answer…Bring him away;
Mine's not an idle cause. The Duke himself,
Or any of my brothers of the state,
Cannot but feel this wrong as 'twere their own.
For if such actions may have passage free,
Bondslaves and pagans shall our statesmen be.
      They exit.

continued on next page

Handout 8.5

From *King Lear* 1.1, 1.2
Speaking Parts: 3

Enter KENT, GLOUCESTER, and EDMUND
KENT   I thought the king had more affected the Duke of Albany than Cornwall.
GLOUCESTER   It did always seem so to us, but now in the division of the kingdom, it appears not which of the dukes he values most, for equalities are so weighed that curiosity in neither can make choice of either's moiety.
KENT   Is not this your son, my lord?
GLOUCESTER   His breeding, sir, hath been at my charge. I have so often blushed to acknowledge him that now I am brazed to 't.
KENT   I cannot conceive you.
GLOUCESTER   Sir, this young fellow's mother could, whereupon she grew round-wombed and had, indeed, sir, a son for her cradle ere she had a husband for her bed. Do you smell a fault?
KENT   I cannot wish the fault undone, the issue of it being so proper.
GLOUCESTER   But I have a son, sir, by order of law, some year elder than this, who yet is no dearer in my account. Though this knave came something saucily into the world before he was sent for, yet was his mother fair, there was good sport at his making, and the whoreson must be acknowledged. – Do you know this noble gentleman, Edmund?
EDMUND   No, my lord.
GLOUCESTER   My lord of Kent. Remember him hereafter as my honorable friend.
EDMUND   My services to your Lordship.
KENT   I must love you and sue to know you better.
EDMUND   Sir, I shall study deserving.
GLOUCESTER   He hath been out nine years, and away he shall again. (*Sennet.*) The King is coming…

Exeunt KENT, GLOUCESTER

EDMUND
Thou, Nature, art my goddess. To thy law
My services are bound. Wherefore should I
Stand in the plague of custom, and permit
The curiosity of nations to deprive me
For that I am some twelve or fourteen moonshines
Lag of a brother? Why "bastard"? Wherefore "base,"
When my dimensions are as well compact,
My mind as generous and my shape as true
As honest madam's issue? Why brand they us
With "base," with "baseness," "bastardy," "base," "base,"
Who, in the lusty stealth of nature, take
More composition and fierce quality
Than doth within a dull, stale, tired bed
Go to th' creating a whole tribe of fops
Got 'tween asleep and wake? Well then,
Legitimate Edgar, I must have your land.
Our father's love is to the bastard Edmund
As to th' legitimate. Fine word, "legitimate."
Well, my legitimate, if this letter speed
And my invention thrive, Edmund the base
Shall top th' legitimate. I grow, I prosper.
Now, gods, stand up for bastards!

From *Twelfth Night* 1.2
Speaking parts: 2

Enter VIOLA, a Captain, and Sailors.
VIOLA   What country, friends, is this?
CAPTAIN   This is Illyria, lady.
VIOLA
And what should I do in Illyria?
My brother he is in Elysium.
Perchance he is not drowned. – What think you, sailors?

continued on next page

Handout 8.5

CAPTAIN
It is perchance that you yourself were saved.
VIOLA
O, my poor brother! And so perchance may he be.
CAPTAIN
True, madam. And to comfort you with chance,
Assure yourself, after our ship did split,
When you and those poor number saved with you
Hung on our driving boat, I saw your brother,
Most provident in peril, bind himself
(Courage and hope both teaching him the practice)
To a strong mast that lived upon the sea,
Where, like Arion on the dolphin's back,
I saw him hold acquaintance with the waves
So long as I could see.
VIOLA [*giving him money*] For saying so, there's gold.
Mine own escape unfoldeth to my hope,
Whereto thy speech serves for authority,
The like of him. Know'st thou this country?
CAPTAIN
Ay, madam, well, for I was bred and born
Not three hours' travel from this very place.
VIOLA Who governs here?
CAPTAIN
A noble duke, in nature as in name.
VIOLA What is the name?
CAPTAIN Orsino.
VIOLA
Orsino. I have heard my father name him.
He was a bachelor then.
CAPTAIN
And so is now, or was so very late;
For but a month ago I went from hence,
And then 'twas fresh in murmur (as, you know,

What great ones do the less will prattle of)
That he did seek the love of fair Olivia.
VIOLA What's she?
CAPTAIN
A virtuous maid, the daughter of a count
That died some twelvemonth since, then leaving her
In the protection of his son, her brother,
Who shortly also died, for whose dear love,
They say, she hath abjured the sight
And company of men.
VIOLA O, that I served that lady,
And might not be delivered to the world
Till I had made mine own occasion mellow,
What my estate is.
CAPTAIN That were hard to compass
Because she will admit no kind of suit,
No, not the Duke's.
VIOLA
There is a fair behavior in thee, captain,
And though that nature with a beauteous wall
Doth oft close in pollution, yet of thee
I will believe thou hast a mind that suits
With this thy fair and outward character.
I prithee – and I'll pay thee bounteously –
Conceal me what I am, and be my aid
For such disguise as haply shall become
The form of my intent. I'll serve this duke.
Thou shall present me as an eunuch to him.
It may be worth thy pains, for I can sing
And speak to him in many sorts of music
That will allow me very worth his service.
What else may hap, to time I will commit.
Only shape thou thy silence to my wit.
CAPTAIN
Be you his eunuch, and your mute I'll be.
When my tongue blabs, then let mine eyes not see.
VIOLA I thank thee. Lead me on.
They exit.

Reading Shakespeare Film First by Mary Ellen Dakin © 2012 NCTE.

Handout 8.6. Character Chart

Inside Outsiders	What causes this character to be perceived as different, dangerous, or despised?	What effect does an outsider's status have on this character? How does this character respond in this scene?
Katherine	A shrew is a nagging woman with a bad temper. Since Katherine is labeled a shrew, she must be considered different from other women—stubborn, witty, sarcastic, disobedient, outspoken, and labeled as unfit to be a wife.	She seems alone, with no help from men or women. In this scene, she seems psychologically confused and broken, treated like a dog that obeys her master's commands. But could it be an act? Maybe she and Petruchio are playing parts in public that aren't true in private.
Caliban		
Shylock		
Hermione		
Othello		
Edmund		
Viola		

Reading Shakespeare Film First by Mary Ellen Dakin © 2012 NCTE.

Handout 8.7. Character Chart: Compendium of Student Notes

Inside Outsiders	*What causes this character to be perceived as different, dangerous, or despised?*	*What effect does an outsider's status have on this character? How does this character respond in this scene?*
Katherine	A shrew is a nagging woman with a bad temper. Since Katherine is labeled a shrew, she must be considered different from other women—stubborn, witty, sarcastic, disobedient, outspoken, and labeled as unfit to be a wife.	Kate seems alone, with no help from men or women. In this scene, she seems psychologically confused and broken, treated like a dog that obeys her master's commands. But could it be an act? Maybe she and Petruchio are playing parts in public that aren't true in private.
Caliban	Caliban is different because of his appearance and his heritage. He might be of mixed race; his mother was an Algierian witch; he's not noble like the Europeans; he's at the bottom of society, a slave and a suspected criminal. His intelligence, youth, and strength make him a threat.	Caliban's status has had a negative effect on him—he used to be happy but now he suffers constantly. He resents his education and wishes he could be ignorant. He responds with angry logic and he seems to threaten retaliation.
Shylock	In history, Christians blamed Jews for Christ's death and made them live in ghettos. Shylock is despised because of his religion and his profession: he is a Jewish moneylender in Venice, a center of the Christian economy.	Shylock has lost everything and he's furious. He argues in public that he is equal to Christians, and he plans to seek justice. But his response is extreme—he will revenge, torture, plague Antonio. Maybe he doesn't care anymore.
Hermione	Being a pregnant queen should be a positive thing but Hermione is despised by her jealous king because he thinks her babies were fathered by another king. This is adultery and treason, a betrayal of king and country.	Hermione seems shocked but strong. She says she is different from other women and they won't see her cry but her grief is terrible. She responds with confidence (is it real?) that she will be found innocent and leaves for jail like a queen, not a prisoner.
Othello	Othello is different because he is a noble Moor, born African and Muslim, and a general in Christian Venice. His marriage is mixed-race. He is powerful but his power might be resented, his loyalty doubted, by the insiders.	Othello doesn't act like an outsider. He seems sure of himself. If he weren't he wouldn't have married a Venetian senator's daughter without her father's permission. Maybe he's naïve or over-confident?
Edmund	Because his father had sex with a woman who wasn't his wife, and was probably a lower-class woman, Edmund's father is ashamed of him. His genes make him different and possibly a threat to his father's reputation or wealth.	Edmund is quiet when his father says how ashamed he is of him. But when he's alone, he questions his status. He seems alienated from family and society; he plans to take his father's love away from his legitimate brother for spite or revenge.
Viola	Viola is a young female alone in a foreign place that might be hostile to her homeland.	Viola seems vulnerable but educated, and asks lots of questions then makes a plan to pass herself off as a eunuch, a castrated male, and serve a local Duke. If she poses no threat to anyone, then maybe no one will threaten her.

Reading Shakespeare Film First by Mary Ellen Dakin © 2012 NCTE.

Handout 8.8. Project Role Sheet

Stage 1: Literary Roles	Stage 2: Theatrical Roles	Stage 3: Cinematic Roles
Discussion Leader: Your job is to keep your team focused on the **discussion topics** and to ask probing **questions**. When your team cannot understand or agree on something in the scene or outside of it (for example, questions about context), **research** potential sources of information (reference books, teachers, etc.) and inform your team. **Annotate** the scene, adding notes about characters and conflict, theme, mood, tone, language and line delivery.	**Director**: Your job is to articulate your team's **objectives** in the scene, write **directorial commentary**, and **storyboard** the scene for a film performance. During scene rehearsals, **coach** the actors in their line delivery; consult frequently with the camera operator. In preparation for the interview, **contact** the expert(s) and arrange a time and place for the interview. **Scout** the location of the interview with the camera operator and decide on the best use of the space and the camera before and during the interview.	**Director**: Your job is to work closely with the film editor to convey your team's **objectives** and **document** the process your team underwent to transmediate a Shakespeare scene from literary to theatrical and cinematic text. **View** the raw footage with your team, sketch a **storyboard** of the shots you consider most essential to the docudrama and the approximate sequence in which the shots should appear.
Director: Your job is to participate in each day's discussion and listen very closely to your team's comments on the characters, conflict, and language and to incorporate the best ideas into a **working script** for a film performance of your scene. This can include line **editing** and ideas for camera work.	**Actors**: Great Shakespeare actors are great Shakespeare readers first. Your job is to **speak** Shakespeare's scene with increasing clarity and conviction. Between readings, work closely with the director, discussing how you should **block** the scene. **Discuss** locations that would contribute to the meaning, mood, and action.	**Editor**: Working closely with the director and the current draft of the storyboard, your job is to **assemble** the first draft shot sequence, cut together in the right order but without the addition of visual transitions (fades, wipes, etc.), title shots, music, sound effects, and/or voice-overs. This is called a **rough cut**.
Readers: Your job is to **read closely** and **interpret** the text, unlocking the language, characters, conflicts, and themes. Read actively: question, clarify, summarize, predict, and connect. Who are these characters? What are they doing? How would you translate their dialogue into modern English? How does the theme impact the meaning, mood, and tone? Your reading sets the stage for the rest of the project.	**Interviewer**: After your team secures one or more experts, your job is to write probing **questions** generated by the scene for the expert(s) that draw upon their background knowledge. For example, if an expert teaches psychology, your questions could focus on the psychological makeup of a character. During the interview, **listen** closely to the expert's answers, because these answers may generate interesting follow-up questions.	With input from the director, you will edit the rough cut into a **final cut**, trimming shots and scenes down to their most essential length. Add titles and intertitles, music, and appropriate visual transitions besides the common cut. Add voice-over narration.
Camera Operator: Your job is to **film the daily conversations**, relying on eye-level medium shots but also using a variety of camera shots and angles that establish the location and focus on team members and the roles each plays. **Audio** is very important—make sure that the human voice can be clearly heard over environmental noises.	**Camera Operator**: Your job is to work closely with the director and to **film** the rehearsals and performance creatively. Film the interview inconspicuously, recording without distracting.	Ready the final cut for **export** and viewing.

Reading Shakespeare Film First by Mary Ellen Dakin © 2012 NCTE.

Handout 8.9. Reading Shakespeare onto Film:
The Production Storyboard

SHOT # _____

Subject:

Location:

Vocal Sound: *What lines will viewers hear? Copy the lines. Will this be a voice-over?*

Nonvocal Sound: *Environmental, music, silence*

Camera Shot Type: **Camera Angle:**

Camera Movement: **Editing Technique:** *Most often a CUT*

SHOT # _____

Subject:

Location:

Vocal Sound: *What lines will viewers hear? Copy the lines. Will this be a voice-over?*

Nonvocal Sound: *Environmental, music, silence*

Camera Shot Type: **Camera Angle:**

Camera Movement: **Editing Technique:**

Reading Shakespeare Film First by Mary Ellen Dakin © 2012 NCTE.

Handout 8.10. Transmediating Shakespeare: Production Project Rubric Template

Criteria	Objectives	Rating
The Story of the Project:		*Excellent? Proficient? Adequate? Inconsistent? Inadequate?*
The Performance of the Scene:		
The Camera Work:		
The Editing:		
The Sound:		

Reading Shakespeare Film First by Mary Ellen Dakin © 2012 NCTE.

Handout 8.11. Final Project Rubric

Company Members:
Play Title, Act and Scene:

Criteria	Objectives	Rating
The Story: **Narrative** **Organization** **Purpose**	➤Tells an interesting and coherent story of the process of transmediating Shakespeare from literary to theatrical and cinematic texts. ➤Documents a creative process of group reading, group discussion, scene rehearsal, interviews, performance, filming, and reflection. ➤Demonstrates growth in reading, questioning, visualizing, speaking, and performing Shakespeare. ➤Engages the audience in the challenge of understanding and communicating Shakespeare. ➤Communicates the complex dynamics of group work, location, problem-solving, technology, and deadlines.	*Exemplary?* *Proficient?* *Adequate?* *Inconsistent?* *Inadequate?*
The Scene: **Line Delivery** **Blocking** **Location**	➤Shakespeare's lines are spoken with clarity and conviction and demonstrate evidence of extensive rehearsal. Lines may be memorized. ➤Lines are accompanied by appropriate movement, gesture, and facial expressions that lend meaning and power to words. ➤Locations are carefully chosen for their relevance to the scene.	
Camera Work	➤Captures and enhances the action, characterization, mood, and theme through a carefully planned and varied combination of framing / camera shots, camera angles, lighting, and camera movement. ➤Demonstrates control, even of handheld moving shots. ➤Emulates the model, Al Pacino's *Looking for Richard*.	
Editing: **Shot Sequence** **Techniques** **Titles**	➤Shot sequence is creatively logical, establishing a beginning, middle, and end that is coherent, fresh, and unpredictable. ➤Editing rhythm (shot lengths) is varied and well paced. ➤Editing techniques (cuts, fades, and dissolves) effectively convey energy, connections between shots, and the passing of time. ➤Titles and intertitles are used to identify people and events, or to provide information and context.	
Sound	➤Vocal sound—a combination of conversation, line delivery, and voice-overs—is consistently audible, appropriate, and effective. ➤Environmental sounds do not distract but contribute to the authenticity of the scenes. ➤Music, if used, contributes to the story, scene, and/or theme. ➤Silence, if used for effect, reinforces the visual design.	

Reading Shakespeare Film First by Mary Ellen Dakin © 2012 NCTE.

Handout 8.12. Final Reflection

A Taxonomy of Reflection
Creating: *What can I do next?*
Evaluating: *How well did I do?*
Analyzing: *What parts did I play?*
Applying: *What old knowledge did I use? What new knowledge will I use again?*
Understanding: *What did I learn?*
Remembering: *What did I do? What did I discover?*

Exhale. Celebrate. Vent. Reflect. Give back.

What did we learn?

This project, and all the weeks and months that led up to it, felt like a journey, so the last thing I will ask you to do is to look back on the process and map a route for the future. Please answer, in any order, as many of these questions as you can.

REMEMBERING
What was this project about? What surprised me most about this project?

UNDERSTANDING
What did I struggle with in this project? What do I understand now—about Shakespeare, about others, and about myself, that I didn't understand before? What did I learn about reading and performing Shakespeare? What did I learn about camera work, sound, and editing? What would I do differently next time?

APPLYING
When did I do work like this before? Are there ways to use or adapt what I have learned about reading Shakespeare as literary, theatrical, and cinematic text to other authors, other assignments, or classes other than an English class?

ANALYZING
What specific responsibilities did I have in this project? What strategies did I use to accomplish my responsibilities? Was there a time when I had to rely on someone else in order to complete my responsibilities? How did I feel about that?

EVALUATING
What am I proudest of? What problems came up that I helped to solve? What can I do better next time? Is this a worthwhile project? How can it be better?

CREATING
How can I adapt what I have learned in this project and in this course to other classes? How can I use what I have learned in this project to achieve the goals I have set and the dreams that I have for my future?

Reading Shakespeare Film First by Mary Ellen Dakin © 2012 NCTE.

Notes

1. According to Carolyn Jess-Cooke, "Montage differs from editing insofar as it is often an isolated sequence of rapidly successive shots that generally provide condensed narrative information" (72).

2. In Handout 2.1 under **Final Viewings,** the average number of words per play (22,594.7) is calculated from "Shakespeare's Text Statistics" found at the OpenSourceShakespeare website, edited by Eric M. Johnson.

3. For a helpful discussion of graphics in film, see Chapter 2 of *Anatomy of Film* by Bernard F. Dick.

Works Cited

Almereyda, Michael. *William Shakespeare's* Hamlet: *A Screenplay Adaptation.* London: Faber, 2000. Print.

Alperen, Timothy. "Edition Covers." Message to Mary Ellen Dakin. 7 Oct. 2011. Email.

Anderson, Lorin W., and David R. Krathwohl, eds. *A Taxonomy for Learning, Teaching, and Assessing: A Revision of Bloom's Taxonomy of Educational Objectives.* New York: Longman, 2001. Print.

Anonymous. Dir. Roland Emmerich. Columbia Pictures, 2011. Film.

Bain, Elspeth, Jonathan Morris and Rob Smith, eds. *Cambridge School Shakespeare:* King Lear. Cambridge, Eng.: Cambridge UP, 1996. Print.

Barsam, Richard, and Dave Monahan. *Looking at Movies: An Introduction to Film.* 3rd ed. New York: Norton, 2010. Print.

Bartels, Emily C. "Shakespeare to the People." *Performing Arts Journal* 19.1 (1997): 58–60. Print.

Bate, Jonathan. *The Genius of Shakespeare.* London: Picador, 1997. Print.

Blacker, Irwin R. *The Elements of Screenwriting: A Guide for Film and Television Writing.* New York: MacMillan, 1986. Print.

Buchanan, Judith. *Shakespeare on Film.* Harlow, Eng.: Longman, 2005. Print.

Bucolo, Joe. "The Bard in the Bathroom: Literary Analysis, Filmmaking, and Shakespeare." *English Journal* 96.6 (2007): 50–55. Print.

"Buzz." *Urban Dictionary.* Urban Dictionary LLC, 23 Apr. 2009. Web. 7 May 2011.

Cabat, Joshua H. "'The Lash of Film': New Paradigms of Visuality in Teaching Shakespeare." *English Journal* 99.1 (2009): 56–57. Print.

Cartmell, Deborah. *Interpreting Shakespeare on Screen.* Houndmills, Eng.: Macmillan, 2000. Print.

Common Core State Standards Initiative. *Common Core State Standards for English Language Arts and Literacy in History/Social Studies, Science, and Technical Subjects.* National Governors Association Center for Best Practices (NGA Center) and Council of Chief State School Officers (CCSSO), 2011. Web. 16 Mar. 2011.

Cook, Patrick J. *Cinematic* Hamlet: *The Films of Olivier, Zeffirelli, Branagh, and Almereyda.* Athens: Ohio UP, 2011. Print.

Coriolanus. Dir. Ralph Fiennes. Hermetof Pictures. 2011. Film.

Costanzo, William. V. *Great Films and How to Teach Them.* Urbana, IL: NCTE, 2004. Print.

Crowl, Samuel. *Shakespeare and Film.* New York: Norton, 2008. Print.

Dakin, Mary Ellen. *Reading Shakespeare with Young Adults.* Urbana, IL: NCTE, 2009. Print.

Dick, Bernard F. *Anatomy of Film.* 6th ed. Boston: Bedford/St. Martin's, 2010. Print.

Eliot, T. S. *Four Quartets.* Orlando, FL: Harcourt, 1971. Print.

Foster, Thomas C. *How to Read Literature like a Professor: A Lively and Entertaining Guide to Reading between the Lines.* New York: Harper, 2003. Print.

Golden, John. "Literature into Film (and Back Again): Another Look at an Old Dog." *English Journal* 97.1 (2007): 24–30. Print.

———. *Reading in the Dark: Using Film as a Tool in the English Classroom.* Urbana, IL: NCTE, 2001. Print.

Hamlet. Dir. Michael Almereyda. Miramax, 2000. Film.

Hamlet. Dir. Kenneth Branagh. Warner Brothers, 1996. Film.

Hamlet. Dir. Laurence Olivier. Two Cities, 1948. Film.

Hamlet. Dir. Franco Zeffirelli. Warner Brothers, 1990. Film.

Henry V. Dir. Kenneth Branagh. MGM, 1989. Film.

Henry V. Dir. Laurence Olivier. MGM, 1944. Film.

Honthaner, Eve Light. *The Complete Film Production Handbook.* 4th ed. Burlington, MA: Focal Press, 2010. Print.

International Reading Association and National Council of Teachers of English. *Standards for the English Language Arts.* Newark, DE: IRA; Urbana, IL: NCTE, 1996. Print.

Jess-Cooke, Carolyn. *Shakespeare on Film: Such Things as Dreams are Made Of.* London: Wallflower, 2007. Print.

Jockers, Matthew L. "Machine-Classifying Novels and Plays by Genre." Blog. Stanford U, 13 Feb. 2009. Web. 13 June 2011.

Johnson, Eric M., ed. "Shakespeare Text Statistics." *Open Source Shakespeare.* George Mason U, n.d. Web. 21 May 2011.

Kajder, Sara. *Adolescents and Digital Literacies: Learning Alongside Our Students.* Urbana, IL: NCTE, 2010. Print.

Kelly, Dianne K. *In Students' Words: The Development of Student Attitudes toward Mathematics—A Social Perspective.* Diss. U of Massachusetts-Boston, 2011. Print.

King Lear. Dir. Trevor Nunn. PBS, 2008. Film.

Krueger, Ellen, and Mary T. Christel. *Seeing and Believing: How to Teach Media Literacy in the English Classroom.* Portsmouth, NH: Boynton/Cook-Heinemann, 2001. Print.

Kuhns, William, and Robert Stanley. *Exploring the Film.* Dayton: Pflaum, 1968.

LoMonico, Michael. *The Shakespeare Book of Lists: The Ultimate Guide to the Bard, His Plays, and How They've Been Interpreted (and Misinterpreted) through the Ages.* Franklin Lakes, NJ: New Page, 2001. Print.

Looking for Richard. Dir. Al Pacino. Twentieth Century Fox, 1996. Film.

Lunsford, Andrea A., John J. Ruszkiewicz, and Keith Walters. *Everything's an Argument*. 5th ed. Boston: Bedford/St. Martin's, 2010. Print.

Macbeth. Dir. Rupert Goold. PBS, 2010. Film.

Macbeth. Dir. Roman Polanski. Columbia Pictures, 1971. Film.

Macbeth. Dir. Orson Welles. Mercury Productions, 1948. Film.

McCormick, Jennifer. "Transmediation in the Language Arts Classroom: Creating Contexts for Analysis and Ambiguity." *Journal of Adolescent and Adult Literacy* 54.8 (2011): 579–87. Print.

McDonald, Russ. *The Bedford Companion to Shakespeare: An Introduction with Documents*. 2nd ed. Boston: Bedford/St. Martin's, 2001. Print.

Mellor, Bronwyn. *Reading* Hamlet. Urbana, IL: NCTE, 1999. Print. The NCTE Chalkface Series.

The Merchant of Venice. Dir. Michael Radford. Sony Pictures Classics, 2004. Film.

A Midsummer Night's Dream. Dir. Michael Hoffman. Twentieth Century Fox, 1999. Film.

A Midsummer Night's Dream. Dir. James Lapine. PBS, 1982. Film.

A Midsummer Night's Dream. Dir. Max Reinhardt and William Dieterle. Warner Brothers, 1935. Film.

Much Ado about Nothing. Dir. Kenneth Branagh. Renaissance Films, 1993. Film.

"Mirror Neurons." Narr. Robert Krulwich. *Nova*. PBS. WGBH, Boston, 25 Jan. 2005. Web. 16 July 2011. Transcript.

Norman, Marc, and Tom Stoppard. *Shakespeare in Love: A Screenplay*. New York: Hyperion, 1998. Print.

O. Dir. Tim Blake Nelson. Lions Gate, 2001. Film.

Othello. Dir. Trevor Nunn. Primetime Television, 1990. Film.

Othello. Dir. Oliver Parker. Warner Brothers, 1995. Film.

Othello. Dir. Orson Welles. Mercury Productions, 1952. Film.

Pappas, Peter. "A Taxonomy of Reflection: Critical Thinking for Students, Teachers, and Principals (Part 1)." Blog. *Copy/Paste*. 4 Jan. 2010. Web. 2 Feb. 2012.

Pearce, Craig, and Baz Luhrmann. *William Shakespeare's* Romeo and Juliet. *Drew's Script-O-Rama*. 6 Oct. 1995. Web. 3 Aug. 2010. Final Shooting Script.

Post, Tom. "Bits and the Bard." *Forbes.com*. 8 June 2011. Web. 11 June 2011.

Richard III. Dir. Richard Loncraine. Mayfair Entertainment, 1995. Film.

Rief, Linda. "Writing: Commonsense Matters." *Adolescent Literacy: Turning Promise into Practice*. Ed. Kylene Beers, Robert E. Probst, and Linda Rief. Portsmouth, NH: Heinemann, 2007. 189–208. Print.

Romeo and Juliet. Dir. Franco Zeffirelli. Paramount, 1968. Film.

Rosenbaum, Ron. *The Shakespeare Wars: Clashing Scholars, Public Fiascoes, Palace Coups*. New York: Random, 2006. Print.

Rosenblatt, Louise M. *Literature as Exploration*. 5th ed. New York: MLA, 1995. Print.

Roskelly, Hephzibah, and David A. Jolliffe. *Everyday Use: Rhetoric at Work in Reading and Writing*. New York: Pearson, Longman, 2009. Print.

Rothwell, Kenneth S. *A History of Shakespeare on Screen: A Century of Film and Television*. 2nd ed. Cambridge, Eng.: Cambridge UP, 2004. Print.

Scott-Douglass, Amy. *Shakespeare Inside: The Bard behind Bars*. London: Continuum, 2007. Print.

Shakespeare behind Bars. Dir. Hank Rogerson. Philomath, 2005. Film.

Shakespeare in Love. Dir. John Madden. Universal, 1998. Film.

Shakespeare, William. *Hamlet*. New Folger Library Shakespeare ed. Ed. Barbara A. Mowat and Paul Werstine. New York: Washington Square Press, 1992. Print.

———. *Henry V*. New Folger Library Shakespeare ed. Ed. Barbara A. Mowat and Paul Werstine. New York: Washington Square Press, 1995. Print.

———. *King Lear*. New Folger Library Shakespeare ed. Ed. Barbara A. Mowat and Paul Werstine. New York: Simon, 2009. Print.

———. *Macbeth*. New Folger Library Shakespeare ed. Ed. Barbara A. Mowat and Paul Werstine. New York: Washington Square Press, 1992. Print.

———. *The Merchant of Venice*. New Folger Library Shakespeare ed. Ed. Barbara A. Mowat and Paul Werstine. New York: Simon, 2009. Print.

———. *A Midsummer Night's Dream*. New Folger Library Shakespeare ed. Ed. Barbara A. Mowat and Paul Werstine. New York: Washington Square Press, 1993. Print.

———. *Othello*. New Folger Library Shakespeare ed. Ed. Barbara A. Mowat and Paul Werstine. New York: Washington Square Press, 1993. Print.

———. *Romeo and Juliet*. New Folger Library Shakespeare ed. Ed. Barbara A. Mowat and Paul Werstine. New York: Washington Square Press, 1992. Print.

———. *The Taming of the Shrew*. New Folger Library Shakespeare ed. Ed. Barbara A. Mowat and Paul Werstine. New York: Washington Square Press, 1992. Print.

———. *The Tempest*. New Folger Library Shakespeare ed. Ed. Barbara A. Mowat and Paul Werstine. New York: Washington Square Press, 1993. Print.

———. *Twelfth Night*. New Folger Library Shakespeare ed. Ed. Barbara A. Mowat and Paul Werstine. New York: Washington Square Press, 1993. Print.

————. *The Winter's Tale*. New Folger Library Shakespeare ed. Ed. Barbara A. Mowat and Paul Werstine. New York: Simon, 2009. Print.

Sharff, Stefan. *The Elements of Cinema: Toward a Theory of Cinesthetic Impact*. New York: Columbia UP, 1982. Print.

Teasley, Alan B., and Ann Wilder. *Reel Conversations: Reading Films with Young Adults*. Portsmouth: Boynton/Cook-Heinemann, 1997. Print.

The Tempest. Dir. Julie Taymor. Miramax, 2010. Film.

Theodosakis, Nikos. *The Director in the Classroom: How Filmmaking Inspires Learning*. Rev. ed. Penticton, BC, Can.: Nikos Theodosakis, 2009. Print.

Thomas, Lewis. *The Lives of a Cell: Notes of a Biology Watcher*. New York: Penguin, 1974. Print.

Thompson, Kristin. *Storytelling in the New Hollywood: Understanding Classical Narrative Technique*. Cambridge, MA: Harvard UP, 1999. Print.

Throne of Blood. Dir. Akira Kurosawa. Toho, 1957. Film.

"Trailer (film)." *Wikipedia, The Free Encyclopedia*. Wikimedia Foundation, 15 May 2011. Web. 17 May 2011.

Twelfth Night. Dir. Trevor Nunn. 1996. Film.

William Shakespeare's Romeo + Juliet. Dir. Baz Luhrmann. Twentieth Century Fox, 1996. Film.

Williamson, Lynette. "Virtual Seating in the Globe Theatre: Appreciating Film Adaptations of Shakespeare's Plays." *English Journal* 99.1 (2009): 71–73. Print.

Witmore, Michael. *Shakespearean Metaphysics*. London: Continuum, 2008. Print.

Yankee, Ken. "Questions for the expert." Message to Althea Terenzi and Mary Ellen Dakin. 20 Jan. 2011. Email.

Index

Author

Photo by Jennifer Cimino

Mary Ellen Dakin, a National Board Certified Teacher, has taught English language arts since 1987 in both private and public secondary schools. A fellowship at the Folger Shakespeare Library in 1994 sparked her passion for exploring innovative ways to teach Shakespeare's plays, and since that time she has presented workshops on teaching Shakespeare in cities throughout the country. From 2002 to 2006, she was a master teacher at the Folger Library's Teaching Shakespeare Institute. She was elected to the National Council of Teachers of English Secondary Section Steering Committee in 2006 and joined NCTE's Editorial Board in 2011. Her essays have appeared in *Shakespeare* magazine, the *Harvard Educational Review*, and *English Journal*. Dakin's first book, *Reading Shakespeare with Young Adults,* was published by NCTE in 2009.

❧

This book was typeset in Palatino and Helvetica by Barbara Frazier.
Typefaces used on the cover were Trajan and Myriad Pro.
The book was printed on 50-lb. Opaque Offset paper by Versa Press, Inc.